THE YELLOW KITE
& OTHER SHORT STORIES

THE YELLOW KITE
& OTHER SHORT STORIES

One boy's take on life in the early 1960's

RICK CARROLL

Copyright © 2022 by Rick Carroll

All rights reserved. No part of this book may be reproduced or used in any manner without written permission of the copyright owner except for the use of quotations in a book review.

FIRST EDITION

ISBNs

978-1-80227-737-1 (eBook)

978-1-80227-736-4 (paperback)

Author's Notes

During the pandemic of 2020/21, I, like many others, took to writing. I had longingly harboured the thought of writing a novel, and with lockdown forced upon us, now seemed the best time to make a start. But where to start and what sort of novel?

As a child born in the early 1950s, I have always had a keen interest in the decade that preceded it. My parents both had active roles to play during WW2 at home and abroad. Reading through my mother's diaries of the early 1940s gave me the necessary background.

I was fortunate enough also to have some wonderful black and white photographs of that period for reference. The catalyst, however, was a true family mystery that had laid dormant for over seventy-five years. Something that would require research and investigation. This was my inspiration and would form the backbone of my novel.

Writing your first novel is both challenging and rewarding. Often more so the former, as you collate events and develop characters. During this incubation period, as I would call it, I found it therapeutic to take a break every so often.

As part of the therapy and as light relief, I decided to write a short story. Sharing this with my family friends and finding their reactions encouraging and supportive. I decided to continue with several more. All of which are based on my experiences of family life growing up in the late 50s and early 1960s.

Very soon, I realised I had produced enough of these to complete a book. What you have before you then is that book. I only hope you have as much enjoyment reading them as I did writing about them.

CONTENTS

The Yellow Kite: Part One 1
The Yellow Kite: Part Two 5
   A Grand Day Out 5
Sink Or Swim: Part One 11
   The Journey *11*
The Baths: Part Two 17
Summer Holiday Circa 1961 25
Chapter 2: First Impressions 33
Chapter 3: On The Beach 39
Chapter 4 43
Chapter 5: Tinned Beef and Bingo 49
Chapter 6: Gone in A Flash 55
Went The Day Badly 75
The Carrolls Go Camping 1 91
The Carrolls Go Camping 2 97
The Carrolls Go Camping 3 103

The Carrolls Go Camping 4 109
The Carrolls Go Camping 5 115
The Carrolls Go Camping 6.................................... 127
The Carrolls Go Camping 7 143
The Carrolls Go Camping 8 153
The Carrolls Go Camping 9 161
The Carrolls Go Camping 10 173

For Cathy

THE YELLOW KITE
PART ONE

One of the essential items to pack for entertainment on a family holiday, along with a bat and ball, was a kite.

Now I ought to say straight away that we always had some fairly miserable specimens: kite-shaped, difficult to get airborne, and generally fragile beyond belief.

Constructed of fine balsa and ultra-flimsy fabric, one nosedive onto terra firma, and it was usually game over.

Fed up with watching other families proudly flying their superior pieces of kit, Dad had had enough. It was time for action.

As an insurance agent, he had a wide circle of clients, many of whom he was on very friendly terms.

Several of these were ex-military people; one such chap was a former Navy man who, during the war, was attached to the Meteorology division.

Specific to his responsibilities was flying weather kites to monitor atmospheric conditions at altitudes.

These kites were of the box frame construction (canvas sides with an aluminium sprung framework) and very robust as they had to carry instruments for recording weather conditions.

No doubt, on one evening at this client's house, possibly over a drink or two and a chat, the subject of their war involvement led to Dad hearing about this chap's duties. He was telling him about these special 'kites' before adding quite nonchalantly that he still had one tucked away in a kit bag in his Garage.

"Military surplus, old boy," he said.

Taking him out to the Garage, he showed him the large kit bag containing the kite.

Brand new and un-flown with all construction instructions, he generously donated it to Dad.

You can imagine my excitement when Dad bought it home. Too big for the boot of the Morris, it had had to be strapped to the roof rack.

Once we hauled it out of the big canvas bag, we soon realised this was no ordinary child's toy.

This was a serious piece of militaria, of box kite design with two bright yellow canvas sections, top and bottom, divided with spring-loaded aluminium spars. It was very well made.

I suppose it needed to be with weather conditions that prevail at sea.

Once fully assembled, it measured over six feet high and nearly two feet wide. To the outer strut was attached a wire cable joined to what was a very thick fishing line wound onto an industrial-size reel containing approximately 1,000 ft of line, or so we were led to believe.

The reel was then attached to the handled section of a fishing rod. Quite neat.

Indeed, impressive it was. However, the downside was that it was heavy and, as we soon found out, difficult to fly in light winds.

Not surprisingly, Dad and I were keen to try it out. Unfortunately, on several occasions, we attempted to get it flying on our nearby green space. However, the wind was just not strong enough, and despite our gallant efforts of running around like lunatics, we couldn't get it airborne.

In fact, I can remember several occasions when we took it out on picnic days, optimistically strapped to the roof rack, only for it to let us down.

Despite these setbacks, I knew its day would finally arrive when we could proudly blow away those other pathetic kites.

It now resided in the garage, slung in its bag from the joists to save room; it was a talking point to my pals when they visited.

Months passed, and possibly a couple of years when one very bright but blustery summer day, we set off for the Kent coast for a day out.

THE YELLOW KITE
PART TWO

A GRAND DAY OUT

"Tis better to have loved and lost than never to have loved at all."

Alfred Lord Tennyson.

Picture the scene if you can: we are picnicking on a large open grass cliff top on the north Kent coastline.

The weather is bright, sunny, warm, and with a brisk offshore wind. Kite weather.

In fact, several fathers and their children are showing off their miserable specimens, mostly traditional shapes in bright colours with bows for tails, all at a very low height, maybe 50 ft.

"What you reckon, worth a try?" says Dad.

"Why not?" says I.

So over to the car, unstrap the heavy kit bag, and haul it back to where Mum and my sister sit expectantly on the car rug.

With Dad's help, I turn the kit bag upside down,

emptying the contents out to a resounding clanging of components.

This noise immediately attracted the attention of nearby onlookers. Not so much the kite fliers, who are busy engrossed with their toys.

Construction takes a while, not least because we are constantly chasing the paper instruction sheet as it attempts to resemble a kite itself. It is now getting seriously windy.

Once fully built and standing upright, it resembles a yellow telephone box.

Dad suggests he walk off parallel to us about 100 ft and attempt a launch. As he walks away, I can see he is already manfully struggling to contain the yellow peril. However, he stoically continues on, pipe clenched in gritted teeth, until he comes to a halt, a respectful distance from fellow picnickers.

"Careful, George," I hear Mum say.

I have a firm grip on the wooden handle and see the line go taught as Dad, imitating a railway signal, suddenly launches the kite into the air.

In next to no time, it caught the up current of warm air and is climbing fast. So fast, the reel is paying out line very smoothly.

Dad has returned next to me with a big grin on his face. "What about that then?" he asks.

"Amazing," I say.

All four of us tip our heads skyward, shielding our eyes from the sun with our palms as it climbs to about 300 ft and settles.

"Now that's what you call a proper kite," says Dad triumphantly, trying to get his pipe alight between gusts of wind.

We sit companionably on the car rug, proudly watching like parents, "Our Firstborn" doing what it was designed to do.

"Never doubted it would fly once we got the right conditions," says Dad. "Brilliant," I say.

Several minutes pass, and with the wind starting to pick up and the kite still visibly climbing, Dad suggests it might be time to bring it down a bit. The wind direction has now veered around and taken it out over the sea. I try reeling in some line but instead, it continues to gain height and distance, picking up a thermal current.

I look worriedly at the reel and notice less than a third of the line left on the spool. And despite my efforts to hold the handle, it is still paying out more line. We now have a crowd of onlookers. In fact, people have stopped their cars on the promenade and are watching the free show, some with binoculars.

With the responsibility of holding the reel steady and the line almost fully extended, I thankfully passed the controls to Dad.

The kite is now at about 500 ft with a little line left, so we can't have had 1,000 ft to start with.

Suddenly the line is at the end of the reel, and now it's down to Dad's skill and strength to guide it back over dry land.

He stands his feet slightly apart and walks like a drunken sailor towards the cliff edge—pipe in concentration mode.

Before long, he's doing a sort of waltzing run, two steps forward and one to the side. I can hear some laughter from nearby.

"Do be careful, Dear," says Mum, with genuine concern.

Dad is no longer waltzing but running diagonally, but still cliff edge bound. "Do you need some help, mate?" I hear a voice close by shout, and suddenly there are two or three men running to assist him.

They quickly catch up with him and form a type of elementary rugby scrum staggering crablike towards the abyss.

We're not sure where to look, skyward at the ever-shrinking yellow phone box or the men.

Just as we can't bear to look, there is a resounding

crack like a gunshot followed by an eerie silence; even the wind has suddenly dropped.

We all look, mouths agape and skyward, at the rapidly disappearing kite. It appears almost happy to be finally free. "Jolly bad luck, mate," I hear a voice say.

I taste the salt as a small tear trickles down my cheek.

Dad returns with his newfound mates, who are offering suitable condolences. "Hope there's no low flying aircraft about," says one.

"Probably land in Belgium," says another.

"Don't worry, son, I'll get another," says Dad as we pack up and troop back to the car. I know he's just softening the blow.

We did get another kite, but nothing like our flying yellow phone box.

R.I.P. yellow kite, wherever you end up.

SINK OR SWIM
PART ONE

THE JOURNEY

On a perfect summer's day with just a gentle off shore breeze, I am sitting high on the pebbles, a safe distance from the rushing tide.

Putting my novel to one side, I watch some youngsters playing exuberantly in the shallow pools close to the shore.

Their screams of delight were a perfect match for the sound of the gulls gliding serenely, high up, in the cloudless sky.

Shortly they're joined by an adult who gently proceeds to teach them the rudiments of learning to swim.

Observing their growing confidence, I reflect on my introduction to the water.

I guess I was fortunate to have experienced paddling in the sea on family summer holidays as a small child.

However, nothing could have prepared me for what was to come when I started swimming lessons in my last year at primary school.

As I recall, the classes started at the commencement of the autumn term, which accounts for the wet, windy, and sometimes frosty weather that always seemed to accompany our trip to the baths.

A few hours away from academia was normally something to savour. Consequently, the mood of my form was naturally quite upbeat.

Standing patiently in a crocodile outside the school gates, awaiting the arrival of the coach to whisk us away, even the grey and misty morning was doing nothing to dampen our spirits.

Little did we know what was to come. If we had, we likely would have run back to the warmth of the classroom or faked a sudden illness.

After a lengthy wait in the rain, the coach made its ponderous approach towards us.

Like many boys of my age, I had a keen interest in anything to do with transport, particularly what constitutes the latest in automotive technology.

I clearly remember seeing the looks of disappointment amongst us boys as the vehicle finally pulled up at the kerb.

Even our teacher Mr. Lomas was heard to mutter,

"Blimey, where did they drag this one up from?"

What we would nowadays describe as "a classic" was then just old, draughty, and uncomfortable.

Still, we were off on an adventure, so recovering quickly, as kids do, we climbed aboard the coach and made our boisterous way to the seats. These proved to be shiny, slippery, and an instant cause of amusement. They were also very bouncy, as we found out when we set off up the lane.

Bouncing, slipping, and sliding about, we were starting to enjoy ourselves. Someone started singing, and before long, we were all in high spirits.

It didn't last long before our teacher Mr Lomas, who was seated at the front, stood up and told us to shut up as the driver couldn't concentrate.

His intervention wasn't altogether successful as a few at the back carried on, probably failing to hear him over the dreadful mechanical noise.

This prompted him, unwisely as it turned out, to attempt to make his way down the aisle towards the rear and carry out a more forceful request.

Now Mr Lomas was on the short side and spoke with a distinct lisp. When he got angry, as he frequently did, the lisp would get worse, and he would go very red in the face. This made him a figure of amusement to many of us.

Clinging bravely onto the slippery poles that ran from the seat backs to the roof, like a drunken sailor, he had just reached half distance when the coach driver took a sudden sharp right-hand turn.

Losing his grip and unable to keep his balance, he disappeared swiftly and without ceremony under one of the seats.

One second he was a man of authority; the next, a clown in a circus.

The coach was in an uproar.

Slowly and comically, he emerged from behind the seats. Attempting to stare down the grinning faces with as much dignity as he could muster; carefully brushing himself down before silently making his way back up to his seat.

We somehow knew we would pay for this later.

The rest of the journey proved uneventful. Eventually, the driver manfully and, with a distinct sigh of relief, hauled the heavy vehicle into the car park beside the pool entrance.

Finally, and with high expectations, we came to a shuddering stop alongside a shiny new coach with dark windows.

Alighting, I looked up at its windscreen, noticing a

sign with "Saint Beads Private Hire."

"Trust them to have something flash," I overhear a classmate comment.

Indeed. Our old Jalopy looked really prehistoric parked alongside this sleek machine.

However, despite all its faults, over the course of the term, we came to look forward to our journey in this old relic.

THE BATHS
PART TWO

First impressions were not favourable. The building housing the pool formed part of a country estate. Along with the main house, it was built in the 1890s in red brick of Victorian Neo-Gothic design.

Formerly a children's home pre-war, it was now the property of the local council.

Even from the outside, it was clearly suffering from severe neglect. Things didn't improve much as we entered through a side door. The interior looked shabby, with flaking paintwork, rusty ironwork, chips, and cracks on the tiled floor that wouldn't pass health and safety standards today.

The pool itself was pea green in colour and exuded an overpowering smell of chloride; this immediately stuck in your throat, causing you to catch your breath.

A light mist hovered loosely over the water, adding to the gothic horror of the surroundings.

I half expected Dracula to suddenly emerge from one of the cubicles that ran down the length of one wall.

We didn't have to wait too long, as almost from

nowhere, a tall man, I guess around sixty appeared from a far off door.

Tall and of military appearance, judging by his purposeful gait, he wore fisherman waders and carried a long pole in his left hand.

The purpose of this pole wasn't immediately clear. However, we very soon discovered its intentions!

He was introduced to us as Mr Jarrett. Apparently, the caretaker of this establishment but also doubling as our swimming instructor.

We were told by Mr Lomas to decamp to the cubicles, two to each, we had to share, no mixing, obviously; boys with boys, girls with girls.

"Walk, don't run!" he shouted as we reluctantly shuffled off to change.

Timidly making my way towards the changing area, it suddenly dawned on me that no one had seen me naked except my mother and our doctor when he had inspected my chicken pox rash.

That was a few years ago. Now I was nearly eleven and understandably very self-conscious. This in itself would be a new experience.

Fortunately, I was paired with another lad, who, like me, clearly shared my thoughts.

We changed silently back-to-back in the cubicle. Both were relieved when we had donned our trunks and joined the queue at the top of the baths.

Drawing the cords together that supported my swimwear, I felt something wasn't quite right. Looking down, I noticed the label sticking out of the front. Too late to go back and change now. I would just have to hope they stayed on ok when I got in the pool!

We all lined up along the wall facing the pool.

In front of us was a shallow tray of water around a metre square, beyond which was a shower protruding from the wall, already I noted, dispensing a liberal spray of water.

By now, Mr Lomas had left the show, probably to creep off for a quiet smoke in the coach.

Consequently, we had been left in charge of Mr Jarrett, or "Old Jarrett," as he was soon to be referred to.

With a voice clearly used to the parade ground. I had been seemingly correct about his military aura. We were told to walk through the tray under the shower and form an orderly queue, henceforth to await further instruction.

Whether it would have been better to have been at the front and be taken unawares by what next occurred is a question of debate.

I was about in the middle, but judging by the screams,

and that wasn't just the girls, the shower was clearly freezing cold.

Having seen what was occurring, when my turn came, I decided the best approach was to sprint through as fast as I could.

I was not the only one who came to that conclusion. However, it was all to no avail as Old Jarrett grabbed us roughly by the arm and forced us to go back through again.

This truly sadistic approach manifested itself throughout our instructions.

Apparently, the ice bath, as we came to call it, was designed to ensure we were not carrying any head lice or fungal infections before we stepped into his precious pool.

Unlikely I felt, as we were all decent middle-class kids from good homes. And more likely to catch something from his rotten pool.

Once we had all endured this torture and he was satisfied that we were no danger to the pool, he enquired if any of us were swimmers.

This question being met with a dumb silence, he then told us to line up down at the shallow end to await his further instruction.

Walking slowly around the pool, I noticed the many signs:

NO DIVING

NO SPLASHING

PLEASE USE THE TOILET FACILITIES ADJACENT TO THE POOL HOUSE.

We all got that message, but not everyone obeyed it!

Another thing I noticed which bought a shiver to my already cold frame was the pool measurement displayed at the deep end just above the water line.

It was calibrated to seven which I interpreted as feet. Crikey, I thought I defiantly wouldn't be venturing up there.

Gathered in a shivering group at one end, we were then told to use the steps at the side to enter the pool. One by one, we slowly and gingerly traversed the small ladder.

I wasn't sure what to expect from the green and murky water, which could, to all intent and purposes, be an acid bath.

Nevertheless, what greeted me was not unpleasant.

Despite the overpowering smell of chlorine, the water was quite warm, in sharp contrast to the temperature in the rest of the building.

When he seemed satisfied we were all suitably immersed, he then barked out further instructions for us to position ourselves along the back wall and face inwards toward the deep end.

I then found out what the long pole was for, which he used to tap and prod us with, forcing us to form up about a metre apart.

This achieved, and looking like some junior chorus line, he proceeded to lecture us on the dos and don'ts of our swimming lessons.

As if the surroundings and the general state of the place had not been enough, The pleasure he seemed to be taking in telling us about likely gruesome injuries that could be incurred if we failed to obey the rules would certainly discourage us.

Now I know you're probably thinking this all reads like an excerpt from *Tom Browns School Days*, but I can assure you this was the early 1960s.

The middle of the twentieth century. Not the nineteenth.

It was, of course, sixty years ago, and we all know how much times have changed.

Notwithstanding the health and safety aspect, a man

like Jarrett would never have been allowed to be in charge of school children.

I am not making excuses for his behaviour; he was a hard taskmaster for sure, who seemed to relish shouting and, on occasions chastising those who transgressed in "His Pool."

But you have to consider he had seen two World Wars and might even have served in the first; he was certainly old enough to have done.

I heard later that he only had one lung due to tuberculosis, explaining why he was happy to wade into the shallow end to administer commands but never ventured deeper than his waders permitted.

As the weeks went by, and while not exactly looking forward to the lessons, most of what he was trying to teach us slowly sank in. excuse the pun.

I never conquered the "ice cold shower" or the awful cubicles whose doors had no locks and would randomly fly open, usually mid-change.

But after many lessons, God knows how much heavily chlorinated water was consumed. Eventually, I achieved a full pool width without touching the bottom. I even have a certificate somewhere to show for it.

SUMMER HOLIDAY CIRCA 1961
NOTES FROM A SUBURBAN BUNGALOW

July 25th evening.

I am a nine-year-old boy looking forward to that long six-week break from school that we called the summer hols. Endless days spent outside playing cricket, building camps, and generally messing about with your pals.

All those halcyon summer days of sunshine (I guess it probably rained occasionally when we were forced inside to play Monopoly).

The long summer break is punctuated by the highlight of a two-week family holiday to enjoy. It's hard to convey the sense of anticipation. For excitement, it far surpassed Christmas and birthdays.

This year was a bit special as we were booked for a fortnight's stay in a static caravan in Dorset.

Previous holidays had often been in spartan guest houses with fierce landladies who guarded their homes with petty rules, serving uninspiring food with military punctuality. For children and I suspect, adults too, it was hardly a warm and friendly atmosphere.

Lying in bed the night before, the excitement of our adventure was far too much to allow sleep.

Mum was busy stowing the small boot of the trusty Morris Minor with our essentials while Dad secured the family suitcases to the roof rack with rope (this was pre bungee tie era).

Outside my bedroom window, our parents whispered voices adding to the expectancy of adventure, "Have you packed the tin opener, George?"

The journey to Dorset was an event in itself. A distance of some 130 miles had been planned meticulously, courtesy of *The AA Book of the Road, Circa 1960* (essential travel for the modern motorist).

The journey time in those days was a pedestrian 5-6 hrs. with stops for breakfast and lunch, so in order to arrive around 2 pm, we needed an early start. This suited Dad especially, as early rising was a hark back to his army days. Very natural for him and no hardship whatsoever.

Mum, on the other hand, I think was a little less enthusiastic. However, being the dutiful sixties housewife, she didn't complain.

Leaving our home in leafy suburbia, we set off around 5.30 am with a planned first stop for breakfast on the hogs back near Farnham (OS Grid reference

SU911483) on the A31, a distance of some 50 miles from home.

The aforementioned hogs back is a stretch of the A31, which affords panoramic and far-reaching views across the beautiful Surrey and Hampshire countryside. (says *The AA Book of the Road, Circa 1960*).

Perfect for a pullover and brew up, as Dad would have put it.

It was nearly eight by the time we reached the breakfast stop. A brief pause in Epsom for Dad to check the cases were still attached to the roof rack, followed by some heavy traffic on the Guildford bypass, thus delaying us somewhat.

Unfortunately, a heavy mist had come down, so visibility was virtually zero.

Sadly then, no panoramic view to appreciate, just the sight of Mum disappearing into the gloom in search of a private spot for a wee!

But we are British, and nothing stops us from our breakfast, so out with the table and chairs, the cornflakes, bread, butter, and marmalade.

Dad is busy getting the little Calor gas stove going. He a study in concentration, pipe clenched firmly in teeth, matches ready to light the bloody thing.

Suddenly and with an alarming whoomph, "Success!"

Ignition achieved.

Thirsts quenched.

Twenty minutes later, breakfasted, we are back in the little Morris and on our way to our next planned stop in the New Forest. (An area of unenclosed pastureland, heathland, and forest in southern England covering some 219 square miles of Hampshire and Wiltshire, so says *The AA Book of the Road*).

Circa 1960, which I am now attempting to read between bumps and lurches from my cramped position in the backseat.

This was to be my task now for the remainder of the journey, mainly to occupy me and stop me from squabbling with my sister, who was becoming very irritated and bored by this stage.

We have a good run for several miles, nearly nudging 60 mph on one occasion. The little Morris's top speed was an optimistic 68 mph, beckoning and almost in sight on a downhill stretch. Mum is now at the wheel, and she is by far the more enthusiastic of the two when it comes to speed. (Her heroine, whom she often refers to, is Shelia Van Damm, a notable lady rally driver of the period).

Dad has gone very quiet in the passenger seat, a sure sign he is not enjoying the experience. "Careful, Eileen," he says. "You have to watch the brakes. We are fully laden, you know."

Mum just smiles sweetly. She has that slightly wild, carefree look about her.

After an all too brief bit of speed, much egged on by yours truly, we are soon in a traffic jam somewhere outside Alton.

The journey from there takes another 2 hours of bumper-to-bumper crawling (today, we moan about the M25, at least we forget).

Arriving at an open forest space close to the town of Ringwood, the mood in the car is a bit fractious. My sister and I have exhausted our "I Spy" repertoire, the view from the back seat of a Morris Minor being somewhat restrictive.

Dad is still silent, and Mum is now a nervous wreck. Trying to avoid the long tailbacks, we had taken to minor roads without much success. My backseat map reading led us back onto the same road we had left half an hour previously. Miraculously we rejoin the queue four cars behind the one that we had been following originally.

After another half an hour of torture, it is with some relief that we all alight from the Morris and acquaint ourselves with what the Forest has to offer.

Everyone's mood lifts as the sun comes out, displaying the magical light and shade of the woodland. It's so quiet away from the road traffic and fumes—just the occasional dry crack of twigs underfoot.

Dad soon makes up for the lack of car fumes by getting his pipe going (it's banned in the car) and then busies himself lighting the camping stove, always a moment of great suspense. Meanwhile, I help Mum erect the table and chairs while my sister goes off to pick some wildflowers.

Lunch passes more sedately than breakfast. I don't think any of us are looking forward to reuniting with the traffic jam.

It's agreed between the adults that Mum will continue with the final leg of the journey as she says, "Your father is better with maps." I was relieved of map reading duties for the foreseeable future.

The last part of the marathon journey in the car passes in a light-hearted mood, all joining in singing songs from the current hit parade. After several verses of *We're All Going on a Summer Holiday*, excitement is at a fever pitch as we close in on our destination.

Heightened by this anticipation, my sister and I begin

shouting out any signs we see that might indicate a caravan site.

After several false dawns, we eventually see the sign for Sandford Caravan Park.

Finally, we have arrived.

CHAPTER 2
FIRST IMPRESSIONS

"Welcome to Sandford," reads the sign.

Colourfully showing happy families enjoying beach-related activities. We drive into the car park and decamp next to the reception and come to the site to shop. The first thing that strikes me is the abundance of Rhododendrons and Pine trees. These give the site a very Mediterranean look and help to cleverly hide the caravans.

We are warmly greeted by one of the Denison family who owns the site, and on receiving our caravan keys, we are instructed to follow a man in a jeep up through the site to our home for a fortnight. It's apparent that some of the caravans close to the entrance are residential and have a permanent look. Some even have little picket-fenced gardens.

As we progress through the trees, the site opens out more, with several little dusty tracks leading to each caravan.

After a few minutes, we come to a halt next to "Our Van."

The man and Dad jump out, and Dad receives

instructions on where we get our water and how to turn on the gas. Dad nods keenly. He is, after all, a bit of an expert in this field.

Before I know it, the man has jumped back into his jeep and disappeared in a cloud of dust, leaving us all staring up at our new and impressive holiday home. "Well, come on, don't just stand there. Help me get the cases down. Let's get cracking." says Dad enthusiastically.

Later on, having settled in and aquatinted ourselves with our new surroundings, Dad made a cup of tea, and Mum had a laydown. It's time to do a bit of exploring.

I go with Dad to check out the loos and washrooms.

They turn out to be some distance away. Down close to the main building. All are very clean and modern with "showers."

I have never seen a "shower" before, and this new experience turns out to be one of the big attractions of the holiday for me, regularly taking them with Dad even if I didn't need to. Mum had never seen me so clean!

In the caravan, we have our own domains. Mum and Dad have their sleeping quarters at the far end with a pull-down double bed, while my sister and I sleep on the separate seats on either side of the folding table at the front. The middle of the caravan houses the stove, sink, and storage cupboards.

A folding door arrangement also divides the two main sections, thus affording the adults a bit of privacy. Ha, slim chance.

The sleeping arrangements are a great source of amusement, constantly whipping us kids into a silly state. My sister has bought along some of her favourite stuffed toy animals in a little brown case, and part of our night-time ritual is to act out little imaginary plays with them. I give them all funny voices and characters, sending us both into fits of giggles.

It takes quite a while for us to calm down but eventually, we all get some sleep and look forward to tomorrow's adventure.

I wake the next morning to the sound of hissing and a strange smell which turns out to be Calor gas escaping. Dad is busy getting the kettle on for the morning brew. I part the curtain above my head, revealing bright sunlight, and I am suddenly aware I am not at home in my bed but somewhere strange and exciting.

After a few more minutes, I hear the kettle start to whistle, followed shortly by a hand appearing around the folding door bearing a cup of tea.

The day has started.

After we are up, dressed, and eventually breakfasted, it's time to plan our day. Dad's outside with *The Book of the Road* spread open on the bonnet of the Morris.

It's decided that as the weather's good, we will set off for the beach. Planning to go to Studland Bay via Wareham and Corfe Castle.

Soon we are on our way, and the Morris is loaded with everything we might need for our day at the seaside.

It is not long before we are in Wareham, a pretty little town. Exiting and crossing the bridge over the river Piddle (bringing hoots of laughter from the back seat of the car), we see in the distance a ruined Castle high on a hill above the village of Corfe. Just before we get to the village, we take a left turn towards Swanage, and after several miles, we enter the hamlet of Studland.

A right-turn signpost, "To the Beach," directs down a woody land to a car park. Now Mum has an adversity to paying for car parks, always trying to avoid the little man who appears demanding money. Fortunately, on this occasion, she doesn't protest too much as Dad duly coughs up the necessary fee.

We alight from the car but still can't see the sea. However, it's only a short walk down a tarmac road, and finally, we are rewarded with an unforgettable sight.

A long sandy beach stretches as far as you can see. Clear blue water on the distant horizon. I am transfixed.

We kick off our shoes and make our way down the beach, our feet sinking into the warm sand. This is an entirely new and not unpleasant experience for me, having only ever had to cope with pebbles and shingles on previous holidays.

CHAPTER 3
ON THE BEACH

With such a large expanse of sandy beaches, it's not hard to find some space, and soon we selected a suitable spot.

Plonking down our towels (mine, my sisters, and Dad's). Mum has a small folding picnic chair. She likes to be comfortable without sand getting everywhere intimate. Soon we are attempting to change into our swimwear.

Acutely aware of exposing myself, I bravely struggle with towels and trunks whilst keenly watching out for low-flying seagulls.

Mission accomplished, and I am good to go. It appears both Mum and my sister were better prepared, having sensibly put on their costumes under their dresses.

Dad, always the man of action, manages to perform a very expert manoeuvre whilst sitting down, finally whipping the towel away with a conjuror's dexterity, nearly knocking off Mum's sunglasses in the process.

"Really, George, do be careful!"

All suitably attired, all three of us rush off towards the ocean while Mum leans back in her chair, pops her sunhat on her head, and takes out her Woman's

Weekly. No doubt, she was hopeful of a few minutes of peace and quiet.

The first thing that strikes me is how warm the water is as we paddle on the shoreline. It is firm underfoot too.

Soon we are splashing about in the shallows, screams from my sister as she gets a soaking from me.

Venturing out a bit further, Dad proceeds to attempt rudimentary swimming lessons. I had had some lessons at the school swimming baths but found this much easier, and with the saltwater aiding my buoyancy, I quickly started to gain confidence lifting my feet off terra firm and attempting a few splashing strokes. Things go well for a bit until I run out of breath and consume a large mouthful of seawater.

This unpleasant experience brings about much spitting and coughing for a few seconds before confidence is regained, I have another try, gradually, and to my surprise, I find I am actually swimming.

Like gaining your balance and learning to ride a bike, learning to swim feels quite a big deal. Soon I'm rushing up to the beach to tell Mum.

"Did you see me?" I ask.

"Yes, dear," she says. I can't see her eyes through her dark sunglasses but judging by her relaxed pose, I reckon she had nodded off. Feeling slightly deflated, I slope off to the water to join Dad and sister.

After half an hour or so, Dad spots our little chattering teeth suggesting sister and I have probably had enough. At first, we defiantly shake our heads in disagreement but soon, the cold wins, and we finally succumb, trudging shakily back to Mum to dry off.

Whilst sitting with Mum being towelled and sipping warm drinks, we observe Dad. He has already swum into deeper water and is fast making his way out to sea.

I observe him through our binoculars.

Dad is a strong swimmer. After years spent in the army in Southeast Asia before the war, he became very accomplished. Later going on to represent the British Army Water Polo team and win medals.

His powerful strokes soon take him out what looks like miles. Within a very short time, he is just a faint dot on the horizon.

I turn to Mum in alarm, "Where's Dad going?

"Don't worry," she calmly states. "He knows what

he's doing.

By now, Dad's exploits have attracted the attention of one or two neighbouring families.

I overhear a lady saying to her husband. "Reg, do you think someone should call the Coast Guard?"

I grab the binoculars again and, to my relief, see the dot is getting perceptibly larger, and before long, the familiar shape of Dad is heading towards us. Moments later and he trotted up the beach towards us, looking no worse for what appears to me to be a heroic effort.

Dad seems already to be getting a tan, and despite his slightly disappointing woollen swimming trunks, he cuts a very manly figure standing dripping before us. A sort of cross between Errol Flynn and Alan Ladd.

Mum looks up briefly, smiles, and passes him a towel which he refuses, preferring what he jokingly calls his scotch towel method, voraciously brushing the water off his legs and body with his hands.

I observe one of two nearby women glancing at him. He returns them a winning smile before sitting down and reaching for his pipe.

CHAPTER 4

We sit in companionable silence for a while, admiring the view and allowing the salt to dry on our skin.

Dad puffs on his pipe. Mum is busy with her crossword. My sister picked a scab on her knee.

The midday sun blazes down from a clear blue sky. The peaceful silence is suddenly broken by a sharp scream as a small child close by drops her ice cream.

Immediately my sister chimes in with, "I want a lolly."

Mum replies with a curt, "*Please,* may I have one?" and begins rummaging in her bag for her purse.

Passing it to me, I head off with my sister in the direction of the little beach shop. "You better go with them, George," says Mum, whereupon Dad reluctantly gets to his knees, adjusting his trunks.

"Race you there!" he says, and before you know it, we are doing our best to catch him up. It is not easy running on soft sand, and although I do my best, he still reaches the shop before me. "Wait for me!" yells my sister, lagging some way behind.

There was quite a queue, so we had a chance to study the artwork illustrations of the ice creams on the board outside.

After much deliberation, we settle on three vanilla cones and an orange sparkle for my sister.

We eventually reach the front of the queue, and while the man is rummaging down the big freezer in search of an orange sparkle.

I notice a group of little stickers displayed on the window. "Welcome to Studland Bay," they say.

I say nothing at the time, dutifully accepting mine and Mum's cones from the man while Dad sorts out the two shillings and nine pence from Mum's purse.

We walk back as quickly as we can, attempting not to drop our ice creams which are melting fast. I give Mum's a lick, hoping she won't notice.

When we got back, she had a bit of a tidy-up, folding our eagerly discarded clothes into neat piles and spreading out the tartan rug for us to sit on.

While we lick our ice creams, I notice that closer to the shoreline, where the sand is firm, children are building sandcastles.

As soon as I finish, I am off across the sand with a bucket and spade. Dad follows shortly and immediately takes charge. "Right first, we have to build a moat," he says, taking my spade and marking out a circle the size of a dustbin lid.

"Next, we dig around the circle like so. Then shovel the sand into the middle like so. That way, we can use it for the keep, see."

He speedily shovels away around the circle while I stand back and admire his handiwork.

Once finished, he straightens up and taps his pipe out on the back of the spade before putting it back between his teeth.

"All yours now," he says. "Carry on."

I busy myself constructing my interpretation of a Norman castle, and I have decided to make it look a bit like the ruined one I had seen this morning.

Half an hour or so later, my work is complete, and as I stand back to admire it, I notice the tide has come in considerably whilst I have been absorbed in the task.

Oh, is all I manage to say as the water suddenly sweeps over my toes and into the moat. Soon it surrounded the castle walls, which were rapidly collapsing before my eyes.

"Never mind," says a voice behind me; turning, Dad is holding a plate with a sandwich on it.

"Come and have some lunch," he says. "Thought I would bring it down to you as you looked a bit waylaid."

As we wander back to join the others, I glance over my shoulder and notice that the sandcastle has now completely disappeared.

"Don't worry," says Dad. "We can have another go to build one tomorrow, maybe a bit further up the beach."

We finish our sandwiches and drinks to the peaceful sound of the waves coming closer.

"Think we might be wise to move in a minute, George," says Mum.

No answer from Dad. He nodded off after all that excursion of his marathon swim. After a gentle nudge by my sister with her finger on his mustache, he slowly stirs.

"Yes, dear, I heard you," he says.

We decamp further back up the beach towards the dunes and find a nice, secluded spot.

Mum tells me to put my shirt on as my back is already red. I am soon to discover the downside of too much sun.

The rest of the afternoon passes by lazily, with Sis and me playing about in the dunes. Very soon, with the wind picking up and the sun hiding behind clouds, we pack up our stuff and head back to the car park.

The car park is empty when we return, unlike when we arrived, having had to queue to get in.

Dad unlocks the door of the Morris and says, "You might want to hang back a bit. It's like an oven in there."

My sister and I wait all of 30 seconds before clambering into the back seat.

"Yow!" we cry.

"The seats are burning us."

"We did warn you," says Mum passing us beach towels to sit on.

Mum settles herself in the passenger seat while Dad taps his pipe out on the tyre before starting the engine and manoeuvering the Morris out of the car park up the hill onto the main road.

After a while, I notice Mum and my sister have fallen asleep, but I still keep Dad company with conversation.

We have been following a Vauxhall estate for quite a few miles, and I have been observing the stickers on their rear window.

I say to Dad that the little flag pennants of place

names they have are like the ones I saw at the beach shop. Maybe it would be a nice idea to try to collect one from all the places we plan to visit. Dad agrees, and with our small pocket money allowance each day, my sister and I resolve to instantly start a collection.

CHAPTER 5
TINNED BEEF AND BINGO

Arriving back at the site, we are eager to wash off the sand, so we all troop off to the shower block.

On the way, we pass the site shop and notice a sign advertising nightly Bingo at 7.30 in the entertainment building next to the reception.

Dad says, "How do you fancy that?" We all agree it might be good fun.

Washed and freshened up back at the caravan, I complained to Mum that my back was sore. Taking off my shirt, she administers chamomile lotion to my back and shoulders, giving my skin a pink marbling effect. It doesn't helps much!

"Best keep your shirt on tomorrow," she says.

Dad and I mess about outside with a bat and ball while Mum busies herself preparing our supper.

Twenty minutes later, we are all seated at the little

table in the van, eagerly awaiting what Mum has rustled up.

Tinned food is very popular now, so we are enjoying Tyne Brand minced beef and gravy (On the tin, it says, "heat me and eat me"), along with tinned potatoes and baked beans (tinned naturally).

This is followed by angel delight and tinned peaches. Yum yum. Mum is such a brilliant cook.

After supper, my sister helps Mum with the washing up while Dad and I go to the standpipe to fetch fresh water.

The big water containers are very heavy when full, and it's a fair distance, Dad manages his OK, but I have to stop occasionally to change hands. I eventually arrive back at the van to see my sister grinning at me through the window.

"What kept you?" she says as I climb the steps to the door. "You should try it," I say.

Appropriately dressed - Dad and I in shorts, t-shirts, and sandals, Mum and sister in bright summer frocks - we make our way down to the entertainment building for the Bingo.

The large room has a wooden floor, and rows of chairs and tables have been laid out facing a wooden stage; I can see a microphone and a large barrel with a handle. Behind that, on a long trestle table are a motley selection of items which I'm guessing must be the prizes.

We find ourselves a table for four, quite near the stage.

From where I sit, I can see carpet sweepers, teas-maids, cutlery sets, a toaster, and a few soft toys, including an ugly doll. There is also an abundance of tinned foods, including the obligatory box of Tyne Brand minced beef; the box even has a picture of a cartoon cow on the side.

The room starts to fill rapidly, and a pretty teenage girl appears at our table and sells us some bingo cards. "How many d'want?" she asks.

Mum pays for three cards and a pencil each. "Ta very much," she says and sashays away to the next table.

"She speaks funny," comments my sister, starting to giggle.

"Think she's one of the Denison family," says Mum. "They're from up north somewhere."

"I hadn't actually noticed her accent," whispers Dad, giving me a leering grin.

A murmur of anticipation settles in the room, broken suddenly by a crackle from the speakers on the wall.

A man has appeared who starts addressing us in a similar accent to the young girl, who has now joined him on the stage.

He runs quickly through the rudimentary rules of the game and then declares that we shall be playing first for a line of five numbers, followed by a full house. My sister and I understand the simple rules as we had been given a bingo set for a previous Christmas.

The tension in the room is palpable as he turns the barrel and withdraws the first number.

I get three numbers in quick succession on the top line, followed shortly by a fourth.

I glance at Dad next to me, who gives a thumbs up. You can sense people holding their breaths. Suddenly there is a shrill shout of "Bingo!" from a large lady across the room, and everyone visibly relaxes with audible sighs.

The young girl comes over to check back her numbers with the caller and declares, "All correct, luv." Awkwardly, the fat lady shuffles up on stage to collect her prize. After a brief conversation, the caller hands her the teas maid, which she triumphantly holds aloft like a cup final winner before waddling back to her seat.

Several games pass without any of us getting close to

five numbers, and the prizes are diminishing fast. In fact, we are soon down to our last cards.

With our penultimate game underway, we are all doing well. I have four numbers and am just now waiting for number 24 for a line.

I look across to Mum, who indicates she is also waiting for one number, pointing to her card.

"Two and four 24," the caller says. For a heartbeat, i am in shock. Suddenly Dad is on his feet and shouting, "Over here!" and the young girl is slaloming her way around the tables to where we are sitting.

She picks up my card and calls out the numbers to the caller, who says, "All correct if you like to cum-oop 'ere, young man." My sister stage whispers, "Can you get the Doggy?"

A quick reassuring look from Mum and Dad, and i make my way across the floor to the stage.

I can feel my face burning, knowing I am momentarily the centre of attention. Two small steps, careful not to trip, and I am actually standing next to the caller, who asks me with a sweep of his hand what I fancy.

"The white doggy," I say shyly.

"Pardon?" he says into the microphone. "Thought you said toaster, lad," he adds, trying hard for a laugh. When none is forthcoming, he reluctantly hands me the dog, which I carry conspicuously back to our seats.

When my sister says, "Let's see him," I am happy to pass the dog to her. Actually, it's a very nice-looking dog with fluffy fur and quite a cute face.

The woman at the next table notices my gesture and smiles sweetly. I suddenly feel very proud.

Note to readers. Chamomile lotion was a cure-all found in every 1960s home first aid kit. It never did much good, but the pink hue distracted from the pain.

The prizes on offer were very tame by today's standard. But in 1960, they were considered luxury items.

CHAPTER 6
GONE IN A FLASH

As I recall, the rest of that first holiday to Dorset was one of adventure and discovery. When you visit new places, they somehow retain a certain magic that stays with you for the rest of your life. The trusty little Morris transported us to some delightful places.

Along with the magnificent beach at Studland, which we returned to on several days, we were also charmed by Lulworth Cove, Weymouth, and Swanage, where my sister and I were entertained by the Punch and Judy.

The County had plenty to offer the whole family. We visited Wareham and Wimbourne, satisfying Mum's ecclesiastical interests, plus, a trip to the Tank Museum at Bovington, which both Dad and I enjoyed. At nearly every place we visited during that memorable holiday, we made a point of buying little pennant stickers, which we christened "flashes" as mementos of our travels.

My sister had wanted in on the collecting, so Dad offered to buy them and democratically decided we would take it in turns to receive them. After about ten days, we had both amassed quite a collection.

Naturally, too many stuck in the Morris's little back window would obscure rearward vision, so we chose to stick them on the inside window on our respective sides in the rear.

I had seen how these were displayed on other vehicles and arranged mine in a regular "realistic flag-like style."

My sister, on the other hand, choosing not to follow convention, was happy to continually change hers around to form different patterns, forever taking them down and re-arranging them until they eventually failed to stick.

This irritated me immensely, so much so that it led to quite a lot of fighting and quarrelling.

In fact, it became a game in itself; whoever got in the back seat first would automatically remove the other one's flashes and either hide them or add them to their own collection.

Mum got really fed up with this bickering and finally confiscated them, putting them inside *The Book of the Road* and locking them in the glove box!

I think she must have relented at some stage because they certainly made a re-appearance. Or maybe we found the key.

"Out of the strong came forth sweetness."

{Judges 14814}

Using my nails to scrape off the intricately patterned ice that has formed overnight on the inside of my bedroom window, I attempt to catch a glimpse of the days weather prospects.

Praying for more of the heavy snowfall that has prevented me from attending school for a couple of days the previous week. Regrettably, this week's disruption to my education hasn't transpired. Despite heavy overnight frosts, the roads and lanes are now passable, and things are slowly returning to normal. I am now eleven years old, in my final year at Junior school, and due to make the big leap to secondary education next autumn.

Today is the penultimate Friday before Christmas and is, as such, the last day of term.

Normally, I would have been in a state of high excitement pending nearly three weeks off school, especially sandwiched with Christmas and all the prospects that might bring.

However, before all that can be enjoyed, one event looms large on my horizon. Something that has to be endured. Something I have not been looking forward to for several weeks: the annual school Carol concert at St Paul's.

My mother, being a regular churchgoer, obviously

doesn't share my view. On these occasions, my sister and I, along with my dad, unless he could conjure up an excuse of working late, would be required to attend.

In previous years things hadn't been quite so bad as I had been allowed to sit with my parents and sister in the congregation.

This year, however, my view of proceedings would be somewhat different.

Unbeknown to me until a few weeks previous, the following information had been relayed to us at our school assembly.

Owing to the seasonal flu epidemic and the subsequent illness of several members of the school choir, a number of children from the final year classes would be invited. Ha.

"Invited" to join the choir as temporary members at the forthcoming annual school carol service.

Climbing back into bed and resting my head on the cool pillow, I recall the horror as my name was read out by the headmaster.

What were they thinking? I had no musical prowess. Discounting a few Beatles numbers I occasionally attempted in the bath, my voice was at best rasping, sometimes croaky. No way was I a budding boy soprano.

Enquiring as to the criteria for choosing these extra choir members. It turned out some bright spark had simply suggested they take the first half a dozen names off the class register. This would explain why I, with the surname starting with a "C," had been chosen, while my two close pals Messrs. "Green and Wood," were left sniggering at my misfortune.

Later, having washed and dressed for school, I sit down for breakfast, and whilst absently trickling golden syrup onto my porridge I reflect on the painful rehearsals I've had to attend in preparation for tonight's performance.

Fortunately, I haven't been asked to sing any individual pieces, but there is one tricky section in one of the carols that require three of us to sing some form of descant. Some stupid tra-la-la-fa-le-la nonsense.

How this is going to go, I dread to think. The rehearsals had us in fits of laughter. Much to the music teacher's annoyance.

Eating slowly, I pick up the Lyle's Syrup tin and study the picture of a dead Lion lying on its side with what appears to be a swarm of bees emanating from its belly.

Printed under the picture, are the words "Out of the strong came forth sweetness."

I wonder: who knows, maybe if we non-members try our best, we might even manage to pull it off and sound quite sweet.

"Richard, do hurry up, you'll be late again."

My mother's stern voice disturbs my reverie. Quickly I finish my porridge and, gulping down a glass of milk, rush off to the bathroom to clean my teeth.

"I've put your boots by the fire in the hearth to warm them. Your gloves and scarf are still drying off in the airing cupboard," I hear her shout from the kitchen.

Removing my school Mackintosh from the hook behind the bedroom door, I collect my scarf and gloves from the airing cupboard, noticing immediately that they are still damp from yesterday's snowball fight on my way home.

Gingerly putting on my soggy gloves, I hope Mum has relented from her previous evening's obstinate mood.

One of the major requirements of the members of the choir for this evening's performance is that we all must wear white shirts with the school tie, along with the school uniform of grey shorts and socks.

Now, as the regular uniform incorporates dark grey shirts, this has provided a problem.

I don't own a white shirt.

Now my dear mother could be very stubborn at times. When I informed her about the need for a white shirt to be worn, she scoffed at the idea.

"Utterly ridiculous, totally unnecessary. I'm not wasting money on buying a new white shirt when you have a perfectly good grey one," she had said.

Understanding my worries about not conforming to the dress code, my Dad made a vain attempt on my behalf to get her to change her mind—all to no avail.

I now faced the prospect of being the odd one out, not something I was relishing.

Hovering on the doorstep and offering my cheek for our habitual parting, I enquired again about the shirt.

"I'll see what I can do," was all the best she could manage. Trudging up the path to the road, I considered my options.

Maybe she might come up with the goods. Failing that, I could always fake a sudden illness.

I knew in my heart that this wasn't on. For one, it would be a bit suspicious as I was attending school today, plus I would be letting down the other unfortunate press-ganged choir members.

The day went well. The staff even let us go home a bit early owing to the inclement weather.

Sadly I didn't feel the usual end-of-term euphoria on passing through the school gate, more of a sense of foreboding at the prospect of the evening ahead. In these situations, I always tried to fast forward my thoughts to the next day, like when you have an exam or dentist visit—trying hard to concentrate on how good I would feel when the ordeal would be over.

Arriving at the entrance to our house and in a more positive state of mind, I notice Dad out brushing the front path of snow. Using a broom and shaking salt as he goes, he had almost got back to the front door.

"Hello, son. Good day at the factory?" his usual friendly quip.

"Yes, thanks, Dad. They let us off early for good behaviour," my standard reply

Entering the bungalow, I hear Mum clattering around in the kitchen. Might as well get this over quickly.

She's busy making mince pies, my sister helping her.

"Hello dear, your back early. We're busy here, but if you want to make yourself useful, you can help your father clear the front path."

"He's nearly finished, actually," I reply.

"We'll don't stand around here cluttering up the kitchen; go and smarten yourself up, you've got to be at the church by five."

"Any luck with the shirt?" I enquire tentatively.

"Sorry, what with the weather, I didn't get a chance to get down to the High Street," she replies, casually wiping floury hands on her pinafore.

Observing my look of disappointment, she belatedly adds. "It'll be fine, don't worry. I'm sure you won't be the only one not conforming to their silly rules." As I trudge disconsolately back to my room, I pass Dad in the hall.

"All right lad, you ok? Looks like you've lost a pound and found a penny," he jokes, affectionately ruffling my hair.

"It's just this bloody carol concert. You know how I'm dreading it."

"I know, son, but it's only a couple of hours of boredom, then it'll be over, and we can all come home and relax," he says, offering me a reassuring smile and a gentle punch on the arm.

"Guess you're right, Dad," I mutter, entering my bedroom and closing the door.

I walk to the window and observe the snowflakes blowing gently off the shed roof.

Perhaps I might get lucky. I imagine a sudden freak blizzard intervening. All the roads becoming totally impassable.

Time passes slowly as I lay back on my bed and gaze idly outside at the weather, like a condemned prisoner ever hopeful of a last-minute reprieve.

Later, suitably washed and with hair slicked down with some of Dad's Brylcreem, I slip back into my school uniform.

Concentrating hard on knotting my school tie and looking down on the freshly ironed grey shirt, I wonder once again how many of my pals will be wearing white ones.

The smell of baking permeates the air, breaking my concentration and reminding me that I'm hungry. Taking a quick glance in the dressing table mirror, I check my appearance.

Poking out my tongue for no apparent reason, I pull a suitable face and follow my nose back to the kitchen to see if I can grab a bite before I go.

The mince pies are very hot. I cautiously lift the pastry lid to release some steam.

"Don't go dropping anything on that clean shirt, will you," Mum warns, swiftly passing me a tea towel to tuck under my collar.

It's only a fifteen-minute walk to the church. Those of us in the choir have been summoned by the music teacher to get there early, half an hour before the start to arrange the chairs for the choir and dish out the order of service programmes.

"See you later then, lad," calls out Dad as I pass the bathroom on my way out. His voice sounds slightly muffled. I picture him fighting with his collar stud.

Mum is there half-dressed in her slip, waiting by the front door for my final inspection. "You'll do," she says, giving me a lipstick peck on the cheek and wishing me well.

As I gain the icy path to the gate, she suddenly calls out.

"We'll be there in about half an hour soon as we're ready. Want to try to get a good seat near the front, it's always busy."

The church is a modern structure of light brick with a small tower and wide porch entrance.

Inside is light, airy, and significantly warmer than most old buildings. Obviously benefitting from central heating, it feels almost tropical compared with the outside sub-zero temperature.

Making my way up the left side aisle towards the altar, I see that the choir seats are already being positioned on the left, facing forwards towards the entrance. Slightly raised on a platform, they will give the congregation a full and uninterrupted view of the members' performance.

I recognise a few of my fellow choristers, predictably the music teacher's pets, diligently arranging the chairs in rows.

"You have to hang your coat in the vestry, Carroll," a red-faced boy with a severe haircut pedantically informs me.

I've noticed that most of the regular members of the choir habitually treat us renegades with disdain.

Very unfairly in my book, as we had been given no choice in the matter.

I'd hoped to leave my coat on until closer to the start, anxious not to have to reveal my grey shirt. However, the heat in the building was already causing my armpits to prickle. The last thing I now needed was sweat patches to add to my embarrassment.

Placing my mackintosh on a peg, I made my way back out into the aisle to lend a hand.

Glancing towards the nave, I see several members of the Boys' Brigade band arriving. Dutifully they follow their leader, a balding middle-aged man looking slightly ridiculous in shorts and long socks.

They start to assemble themselves along with their instruments in a group on the right-hand side of the nave.

I understand they are to be our accompaniment. If

their musical prowess is anything to go by, I don't care to imagine what sort of racket they will make. I only hope the organ drowns them out.

"If you want to make yourself useful, you can distribute these out," comes a small voice behind me.

Turning, I'm confronted by a girl of my own age. Her pale skin combined with dark hair and a smile set off with perfect teeth is enough to cause me to blush with embarrassment.

"Sure," is all I'm able to mutter, eagerly taking a bunch of programmes from her.

"Thanks," comes her reply before she turns swiftly and disappears back up the aisle.

Keen to impress, I quickly start to work my way down the rows towards the entrance, placing the programmes carefully along each pew, making sure they don't slide off the highly polished surfaces.

Approaching the rear of the church, members of the congregation are already starting to arrive, each being welcomed by the vicar, who eagerly grasps their hand while engaging them with a few benign words of greeting.

I spot some of my classmates with their parents. All suitable attired in our school uniform, all offering sheepish smiles and encouraging thumbs-ups.

I only hope I can deliver on my newfound celebrity

status. Not that any of them are jealous, mind you. Most are no doubt relieved it's not them who's got to stand up here tonight and make a fool of themselves.

"Will all choir members please come to the front of the church?" The shrill sound of our music teacher's voice rings out, instantly subduing the voices of those arriving.

The church is now filling up fast. Pushing politely past several dithering groups, it takes me a few minutes to make my way back up to the front.

By the time I arrive, I realise that all the back rows of seats that house the choir are already taken, leaving me with no choice but to take a seat in the middle of the front row. Glancing over my shoulder I survey a sea of crisply white shirts.

This is a disaster. It means I will be right at the front facing the congregation. I'd been hoping to hide somewhere near the back, out of view and inconspicuous. Now I'm going to stick out like a sore thumb.

Despondently I sit and slowly watch as the church fills.

The pews at the front are only six feet from the choir. These are now filling up fast, and as the families settle, I'm sure I spot one or two glances in my direction. Even the occasional discrete finger being pointed. As I note their observations, my anxiety builds. Feeling my face flush and my stomach tighten.

Attempting to stay calm, I distract myself by reading the programme. I focus hard on the number of pages, trying to judge how long this torture is likely to last.

Suddenly our music teacher appears and immediately starts to instruct us on when we should stand and when we should be seated.

She seems preoccupied with getting this aspect of our performance right and, fortunately, remains oblivious to one of her member's non-conformist attire.

Satisfied she has delivered her instructions satisfactorily; she walks confidently back to her seat across the aisle

I observe my parents and sister arriving. Dad sees me, giving me a wink and a little wave. They settle themselves in the middle of a pew about three rows from the front. Mum's obviously insisting on getting a good view of proceedings.

Concluding that at the moment, I'm only being viewed by the front row pews, I start to relax a bit, allowing myself the chance to glance across to the other side of the church, trying to spot any other classmates. The organ starts up, its random reedy sounds mixing gently with the low hum of conversation.

I glance once again at my programme, the print now sticky from my sweaty hands.

Not long now to kick off.

We're starting traditionally with *Once in Royal David's City*. Solo for one boy soprano member of the choir followed by the rest of us. Finally, from the second verse, the congregation will join in.

Next comes a lesson, something about Adam and Eve, followed then by this fa-le-la rubbish.

It's at that point that the choir will stand up while the congregation remains seated.

The concert duly begins.

Proceeding smoothly through the first carol with a faultless performance from the choir.

Finally, as it comes to an end, there's a short pause while the vicar positions himself at the lectern to read the first lesson.

Speaking in a gentle Scottish borders brogue, he drones on and on.

What he's saying, I have no idea. I'm too busy trying to concentrate on the words for my forthcoming contribution.

I glance warily across to my left to see our music teacher positioning herself in the aisle in readiness to conduct us.

Further over, the Boys' Brigade is eagerly getting organised.

Soon the vicar has finished, then follows another lull in proceedings during which all I can hear is the rustle of programmes being hastily turned over. Quite unexpectedly, the organ emits a few loud and quite startling blasts.

Surprised by this sudden intrusion, our music teacher frantically lifts her arms, palms up, indicating we should immediately get on our feet.

My moment has arrived.

Reluctantly rising, I immediately feel my knees starting to shake. Trembling and trying not to show my nervousness, I discreetly wipe the sweat from my palms down my shorts. Determinedly focusing my eyes on the clock that is mounted high up on the wall by the entrance, I try anything to distract me from the terror rising in me.

Seconds before the carol commences, I am acutely aware of several faces in the front row glancing intently in my direction.

I also detect a few words being exchanged. Heads bowed, whispering. I'm sure I hear someone mutter, "Such a shame they're not all in uniform."

As the organ pauses briefly and the choir finally joins in, I gratefully raise my arms to head height, allowing the programme to shield my burning face.

Although the choir is now in full voice, I manage skilfully to mime my performance. Giving the impression to those present of joyful singing whilst not emitting any actual sound.

Finally, we arrive at the moment of truth: the section when I and two others will have to perform the ridiculous descant to this piece.

Strangely, as we get the cue from our music teacher, I realise I'm no longer feeling that nervous, only experiencing a numb detachment from proceedings. In fact, far from now, feeling scared stiff, this mild out-of-body sensation encourages me to give it my best shot.

Just as we are about to launch into our fa-le-la's, a loud and somewhat rude sound all but drowns out nearly everything.

This welcome intrusion signifies that the Boys' Brigade has come to life. Thank God for the boys in blue.

With the "Junior Calvary" as my saviour, I decide to launch into the piece with some vigour. Almost now shouting the ridiculous words.

Despite my heroic endeavours I find myself effectively drowned out by their tuneless inharmonious accompaniment. My contribution, thankfully, goes by quite unnoticed.

As the din continues, I observe smiles and much-undisguised amusement amongst members of the congregation.

Entertainment comes in many forms.

Mercifully and not before the time, the mini-concert within a concert comes to a ragged halt. Finally, ending with a discordant blast from an errant bugler.

The congregation is now visibly enjoying themselves. Restrained giggles give way to peals of laughter.

In an attempt to regain a sense of reverence for the proceedings, the vicar climbs the steps to the lectern and, using the strategically placed microphone, coughs briefly in its direction.

To his visible embarrassment, the device only manages to duplicate a similar sound, save for a few octaves higher than the recently departed racket.

This brings about another smatter of laughter, prompting him to raise both hands above his head in a plea for quiet.

Thankfully for those who appreciate the religious and festive aspects of a carol concert, the Boys' Brigade's contributions remain dormant for the rest of the service.

Some, like me, however, enjoyed their brief appearance, adding as they did a refreshing music hall interlude to the evening.

Suddenly I no longer felt bothered by what people

might be thinking of my dress code.

Accordingly, I set about my singing duties with a renewed conviction, belting out the remaining carols in my best alto.

Later joining my parents on the porch, I experienced a feeling of lightness, not of the religious type you understand, but more a great sense of relief at having survived a tricky few days.

Finally, as I lay my head on my pillow that evening, I recall the caption on the tin of Lyle's syrup, "Out of the strong came forth sweetness."

It made me wonder if that had been some sort of metaphor for my experience.'

WENT THE DAY BADLY

"If you tell the truth, you don't have to remember anything."

Mark Twain.

Days out with the family were always a little adventure in the early 1960s.

Mum and Dad had bought their first Morris Minor in 1959, a side valve split screen model with 918 ccs. Finished in black, this 1951 four-door model produced a whopping 29 hp. It had a top speed of 62 mph and a 0-60 of... Well, let's say it was best measured with a calendar.

However, they had recently traded in the old one and were now the proud owners of a 1958 948cc model with 37 hp and badged by Morris as 1000. Boasting an optimistic 72 mph top speed and resplendent in Old English white with a red leather interior, it was my parents' pride and joy (after my sister and me, of course).

Setting a president for all future car purchases, Dad decided to give the new family edition a decent "run."

A trip to the coast was on the cards.

So, one sunny Sunday morning in early summer, we

are heading off to the seaside destination: Cooden in East Sussex, coincidently just a couple of miles from where I am writing this and now reside.

The journey down the A21 was fairly uneventful with Mum (always the speed queen) extending the Morris's lively and willing little motor whenever possible on the straight sections, and before my sister and I have exhausted our cries of "Are we there yet?" or started fighting in the back seat we have arrived at Cooden Beach.

Safely parked in close proximity to the beach access, we unload the car and troop off to find a suitable spot.

Setting out the rug on the pebbles, Mum points out that there is quite a lot of tar about, and we should be watchful where we sit. A pretence of what was to come and, sadly, a message not heeded.

Mum had recently bought me a smart pair of white shorts. Probably an unwise choice of colour for an eleven-year-old boy, but I was starting to get a bit fashion conscious and taking a little more pride in my appearance.

Duly attired in said shorts, t-shirt, and sandals, I felt suitable dressed for a day out to the seaside.

The day passed lazily by, with swims, beach games, and a picnic until, with the inevitable clouds closing in, it was time to head off home.

Changing out of swimming trunks on a pebbly beach

is always a delicate operation, and trying to squirm into my shorts without drawing attention can be a bit of a performance for adults, let alone kids of a certain age; so it's with some relief when I am finally able to stand up to finish dressing.

As I bend down to slip on my sandals, I notice in horror that I have somehow acquired a large smudge of tar on my precious new white shorts.

"Oh no, Mum! Look."

"I said be careful of the tar, didn't I?" she says.

"Only thing that will shift that is white spirit or a drop of petrol," says Dad.

As Mum and Dad get changed, I am already thinking: where can I find some petrol?

Well, the Morris is the obvious answer, so quick as a flash, I offer to take a few items back to the car while the others continue to tidy up. Surprised at my eagerness to be of some use for a change, Dad shrugs his shoulders and throws me the keys.

I hastily make my way up the beach with a plan already forming in my head.

What I need is a stick and one of Mum's tissues which she keeps handily in the glove compartment.

Arriving breathlessly at the car, I see to my good fortune we have parked close to some bushes, and in a flash, I notice a long twig that looks suitable for what

I have in mind.

Quickly stripping off the remaining leaves, I now have a suitable stick of about 2 ft which should be long enough to poke into the fuel tank.

Retrieving a tissue from the glove compartment and attempting to attach it to the stick proves tricky, but with a bit of a twist, I feel I have the right tool for the job.

With a quick furtive glance towards the beach to check for their imminent return, I swiftly undo the fuel cap and dip the stick.

I sense it reaching the bottom of the tank and quickly retrieve it with the result, a suitably soggy tissue still attached.

Well, half-attached, actually, but that doesn't seem important as I can now set about getting this horrible tar off.

I speedily set about the troublesome area with the petrol-soaked tissue only to spread the stain further, now making it look like I have had an embarrassing accident!

With little time to think about what I will now say to Mum, and with the sound of their approach, I fling the stick into the bushes and casually lean on the bonnet, nonchalantly awaiting their return.

My sister arrives first, grappling with the picnic basket.

"Thought you were coming back to help," she says.

"Good exercise," I say.

"Oh, shut up," she replies.

"Now, now, you two, don't start. We have a long drive home, so get in the car and behave yourselves," says Mum.

We oblige. Once Dad has tapped out his pipe, clamping it back unlit between his teeth, climbed in, and adjusted his seat and mirror, we are all set to go.

Dad turns on the ignition, pulls the starter, and nothing. Just a whirring of the starter motor. "Funny," says Dad, "Usually goes the first time."

"You have got the ignition on George?" says Mum.

"Yes," says Dad giving a withering look into the rearview mirror; I think solely for my benefit.

He tries the starter once more, and this time without hesitation, the engine fires, and we are on our way.

At this stage, I harbour no thoughts of what I might have done to cause a problem with the car as I am more concerned about disguising the large stain on my shorts.

I sit with my hand discreetly over the contaminated area more to hide it from my sister, who I know will no doubt dob me in if she spots it.

Fortunately, Mum is in the front and resolutely

scanning the road ahead, so for the first few miles, all is quiet in the car

I look to my right and observe my sister has dozed off, and I am just starting to feel drowsy when suddenly Mum proclaims, "I can smell petrol."

"Can you smell it, George?" she says.

"Actually, now you mention it, Bubbs," (Dad's pet name for her), "I can smell it. Thought it might be when I tried to start the car, it must have flooded it, maybe." I discreetly lower my window an inch, hoping to dissipate the fumes.

Mum immediately swivels in her seat and instructs me to close it as it's causing a draft that might bring on one of her headaches.

We drive on in silence, sister peacefully asleep and Mum probably too, although from where I sit, I can only see the back of her head.

So, everything is quiet in the car, just the regular boom boom of the Morris's little exhaust as Dad decelerates on some downhill stretches. Even the smell of petrol seems to have lessened although we have probably got used to it.

Approaching Tonbridge on a gentle incline, the car gives a little cough and proceeds to slow. Dad changes up to third gear, saying, "That's strange: our old one could take this in top gear."

Before he has a chance to add any more, the car proceeds to lose all power, the engine cuts out, and we slowly coast to a stop just on the prow of the hill. "Well, we're not out of fuel," says Dad, tapping the gauge.

Fortunately, there is not much traffic about, so he pulls the bonnet lever, climbs out, and goes to peer under the bonnet.

"What's up? Why have we stopped?" says my sister, now fully awake. "We've broken down," I say.

"Where are we, Mum?" she says.

"Somewhere near Tonbridge, I think," before adding, "Your father's not a mechanic, so he won't know what he's looking at." However, before she's finished pointing out his mechanical shortcomings, we hear a resounding tapping coming from under the bonnet, followed by a "Can someone turn the ignition on? Right? Let's try it now."

Closing the bonnet and climbing back in, Dad pulls the starter, and the engine immediately bursts into life. A few quick blips of the throttle to confirm all is once again. He offers a brief smile to Mum, and we are on our way once more.

"What was it then?" says Mum.

"The, you know, fuel pump wasn't ticking, so no fuel was getting through to the carburettor. Gave it a tap, and it started, so I knew it would likely start. Strange, must have been a blockage somewhere."

Mum then goes into one about Dad always trying to save money by buying cheap unbranded fuel instead of BP or Shell.

Like she's the expert.

Poor old Dad, he can never win even when he has fixed the problem.

We proceed on through Tonbridge and then Sevenoaks (my parents' hometown), which always gets them reminiscing about some story from their youth. All is calm and serene in the car when very suddenly, the engine coughs once again, loses power, and we grind to a halt.

I estimate we are about 5 miles from home as I can see the familiar café, *The Ox in Flames*, some 200 yards distant.

Dad pulls into a convenient lay-by and goes to climb out but not before Mum has berated him about changing the car and how good and reliable the old one was (despite all the rust, which she conveniently fails to mention).

Dad, as usual, takes it in his stride and proceeds to go under the bonnet to see if he can work his magic again.

Several minutes pass, and many tapping noises emit from the front. Mum fumbles in her handbag for her cigarettes, then thinks about the petrol fumes and puts them away. Time ticks on; this is clearly not a five-minute fix.

Dad's head appears over the bonnet. "Think we better phone the AA," he says. "The café will be open, I expect," says Mum.

He closes the bonnet with a resounding clatter and, with a resigned sigh, sets off up the road towards the café, leaving a trail of pipe smoke in his wake.

He's back in about 10 mins with some crisps from the café, slinging them over the back seat to us as he climbs in the car. "Be about half an hour, they reckon," he says, passing a packet to Mum.

"Mines got no salt in," I say, and Dad passes me the little blue twisted bag from his to share. We munch in silence.

I'm in something of a dilemma: should I own up about the petrol dipping or keep quiet and say nothing. I'm just about to come clean when my reverie is interrupted by the sound of a motorbike.

I swivel round to look out the back window to see the AA man has arrived on his combination. He looks very smart in his brown uniform with leather boots. He proceeds to remove his goggles and crash helmet, placing them carefully on the saddle along with his big leather gauntlets.

Dad climbs out to speak with him while Mum is speedily applying her lipstick with the aid of the interior mirror. Honestly Mum!

Dad lifts the bonnet and is joined by the patrolman who stands in a military manner, hands on hips listening to the tale of woe that's been our journey. "Can I go and watch what he's going to do, Mum?" I might learn something," I say.

"Yes, but stay on the kerb and don't get in their way," she adds cautiously.

I climb out and join the men. Dad's finished giving his detailed mechanical knowledge to the man, who now has his head right down inside the engine. "Looks likely to be a fuel issue," I hear him say.

With that, he straightens up and walks back to his motorbike to fetch the appropriate tools.

Dad is about to light his pipe when there's a tap on the windscreen, and I see Mum wagging her finger.

Dad sheepishly puts the match back in the box and gives me a grin.

The light has started fading a bit now, so the AA man has bought a torch to see down into the engine bay.

I'm wondering what he might find.

He calls Dad over, and now they are both peering down into the void.

"Right," he says. "We have fuel in the float chamber, so that's good, but it looks like there's a blockage to the carb. If you jump in and crank it over, I'll undo the feed to the carb."

Dad duly cranks it over, and I take up a position over the nearside front wing affording me a good view of the procedure.

As the engine cranks over, the AA man unscrews the union connecting the fuel feed pipe to the carb. "No sign of any fuel yet," he says to me. Then suddenly, "Whoa. Whoa. Hang on, that's enough!" he shouts.

I quickly signal to Dad to cease pulling the starter, and he obliges.

"Well, I'll be blown; come and look at this," says the AA man, holding out the palm of his hand for our inspection.

With that, Dad rejoins us, and we all stare open-mouthed at what he shows us.

"Looks like a piece of paper or some such," he says.

My stomach does a somersault, and I feel a bit sick as I stare down at the small white sliver of pipe-shaped paper.

"Interesting I wonder how that got into there," says Dad. I lookaway, not wishing to meet his stare.

"Well, you know what caused the breakdown now, sir. What you'll need now is a three-eighth spanner to undo that pipe. If it happens again, I might suggest you best get the tank drained and flushed just to be on the safe side. Don't know how much of that stuff is still floating around in there."

"Ok, sir, now if you'd like to give her a try," he says.

Dad jumps back in, pulls the starter, and the Morris bursts into life. Dad administers a celebratory bleep on the throttle and gives the AA man the thumbs up, who returns the compliment with a formal salute.

"Well, thanks a lot," says Dad.

"All part of the service, sir," he replies, and without further ado he's climbing astride his motorbike, a neat kick over of the starter, and before we know it, he's swiftly on his way.

"Well, what a nice chap," says Dad.

"So, what was up with it?" says Mum.

"Very odd, Bubbs," he says "A small piece of paper or something in the fuel line, can't think how it could have got in there."

Mum immediately starts on at Dad about the ropey dealer that sold us the car. I'm thinking the time has come to come clean. I can't let him take the rap for this, so as we approach our home, I lean forward between the seats and begin to confess my sins.

Mum goes off on one, which is expected and predictable but what really hurts is Dad's silence.

I just detect his teeth are clamping his pipe stem a little harder.

Footnote: Depressingly, the three-eighth spanner was needed on several more occasions (Dad kept it handy in the glove compartment at the ready). Unfortunately, I always seemed to be in the car when the paper tissue made its unwelcome appearances.

My unbinding memory of those occasions was Dad being very controlled and calm, going around opening the bonnet, doing his thing with the offending bit of paper, climbing back in, and fixing me a menacing stare before gently driving off.

Me Dad and my Sister in our garden in Orpington.

The good Cub Scout. I'm third from left, looking very serious.

Trying our hand at Crazy Golf.

Me with "That Jacket" and my Sister on Holiday.

The Carroll's camping at Pluck's Gutter.

The Carroll family 1956. Pictured at my Grandmother's home in Sevenoaks Kent.

Picnic in our Garden circa 1960.

My Mother "potato bashing" at camp

The Dog and Duck Public House 1990

Dreaming of Pascalé and her Panhard PL17

THE CARROLLS GO CAMPING 1
(aka On the Road Again)

Somewhere around the Mid 1960s, my parents decided to take a break from static caravan holidays and try out camping.

Whether this decision was a financial one or just their spirit of adventure remains a mystery.

However, knowing their like for the great outdoors, I tend to favour the latter. Dad had, as usual, acquired a couple of tents from one of his clients. I think these were probably borrowed as Mum was always very anxious about making sure we didn't damage them.

The remaining camping paraphernalia, camp beds, cooking stove, ground sheets, etc., were all bought new. Everything else needed for a camping trip they probably already had from their caravanning days.

As it was to be our first family holiday under canvas, the decision was taken not to venture too far from home, concluding it safer to stay within our county, bearing in mind the unpredictable August summer weather,

East Kent would be our destination. A campsite in a Pub Garden by the River Stour at the oddly named

Plucks Gutter. Chosen, I suspect, not for its close proximity to several beaches, but more likely, it was cheap.

So, the evening before departure and with an absence of my usual sense of high expectations, I helped Dad strap all the camping gear to the roof rack of our Morris Minor

To kick off, there were two tents in hessian kit bags (suspiciously like Army surplus), camp beds, folding chairs, a cooking stove, and fishing rods (all this on the roof).

In the small boot went our clothes packed in two old suitcases, sleeping bags, and ground sheets.

My sister and I would have to share the back seat with two cardboard boxes placed strategically between us. One box containing food, the other, pots, pans, cutlery, all but the proverbial kitchen sink.

I suspect dividing us with cardboard also had the benefit of preventing us quarrelling with each other on the journey.

I almost felt sorry for the little car as with each added item, it noticeably sank further on its springs. This gave it a sportier stance but probably did nothing for the handling.

Our loading task finally complete, and with dusk upon us, we made our way indoors and readied for bed.

Early starts were always a feature of our summer vacations, and although our destination was a mere sixty miles from home, it was still deemed necessary to be up with the lark.

Lying in bed urgently seeking sleep whilst listening to the steady rainfall on my bedroom window, I, at the tender age of thirteen, am already harbouring nostalgic feelings for our holidays in Dorset.

Saturday morning arrives as Saturday mornings do. Dad is first up as usual. The comforting sound of tea being prepared dispersed with bursts of his familiar smoker's cough.

Venturing from my bed, I pull back the curtains to reveal a damp morning with a strong breeze already in evidence.

Hardly camping weather. My spirits sink. I climb back into bed

Soon Dad is giving a little knock on my door, informing me with a merry "Teas up."

Not wishing to be a killjoy and remain under the blankets,

I throw back the covers and plod off in the direction of the kitchen. Passing through the living room on my way, I notice Mum has put out the breakfast plates and cereals on the dining table in readiness for an early start. All very organised.

In the kitchen, Dad is busy getting the gas grill lit for our toast. He is humming a military tune.

His early morning habitual cheerfulness is much in evidence. "Sleep well, lad?" he enquires with a ready smile.

I mumble a reply whilst carefully side-stepping the cat, who, briefly disturbed from an unaccustomed early breakfast cocks me a cautious look before urgently returning to his bowl.

"Is this one mine?" I say, reaching onto the draining board to collect a mug. "Yes, that's yours, the blue one. One sugar. Your mother's is on the left. Do you want to take it into her?" he says.

With that, the kitchen door opens, and in walks Mum looking slightly careworn. Stifling a yawn and reaching for her tea, she enquires about the weather prospects.

Unsure if she's addressing me, Dad or the cat, I reply with a desultory, "It's raining."

"Any fool can see that," she says, "What's the forecast?"

"According to last night's bulletin, it will start wet then should brighten up this afternoon," adds Dad encouragingly.

"Well, let's hope they're right for a change as I've packed the plastic macks just in case we need them," she says, taking a sip of tea before continuing with,

"Now, did you speak to Mrs Hutchens about feeding the cat and watering the plants?"

"Yes, dear," he replies, giving me a raised eyebrow look before adding, "I hope she gets that in the right order. Cats don't care much for water."

Our chuckles are halted by a serious stare from Mum before she disappears out of the kitchen to go and get dressed.

Dad and I finish our tea in silence, watching the rain increase its intensity, busy making intricate patterns on the kitchen window.

"Clearing up shower," says Dad, forever the optimist. "Hope you're right," I reply.

Dressed, washed, and adequately breakfasted, we alight from our little bungalow and proceed to the car. Mum goes across the road to post our keys through our neighbour's letter box while Dad attends to the ropes on the roof rack. Diligently pulling on each one, in turn, to double check their tightened and we're not likely to lose our cargo in transit.

Meanwhile, my sister and I carefully traverse the

cardboard boxes before squeezing into the cramped rear seats.

"This is a joke; you can't expect us to sit like this? I can't even see out. Look!" says my sister, banging the cardboard boxes with her fist. "That's enough of that. It won't be for too long," says Mum getting in. "How long?" She asks.

"Oh, I expect only for a couple of hours," comes the reply.

"A couple of hours? You are joking! I'm going to be sick!"

She wails, starting to cry.

"Nobody is going to be sick. Now just be quiet, and let's get going,"

"Christ," I mutter.

"Don't blaspheme," snaps Mum sharply before adding, "George, start the car!"

Acting on her command with swift obedience as every good soldier should, Dad promptly selects first gear, lets out the clutch, and we are on our way.

THE CARROLLS GO CAMPING 2
(aka Who Needs a Map Anyway?)

The first part of the journey proves to be fairly uneventful, and despite our car's slow progress owing to the substantial weight increase, we make it to Canterbury by midday.

"Time for a break and a bite to eat," says Dad as we pull into the car park behind the city wall.

Mum alights to find a loo and inspect the cathedral, thus achieving the dual purpose of physical and spiritual relief, while Dad deals with checking under the bonnet to make sure we still have an engine!

Satisfied that all is well in that department, he then proceeds to frantically rummage through the boot in search of the flask and lunch boxes. "Now where's she put the b****y lunch," I hear him mutter.

Shortly after much scrapping and shifting of luggage, he finally returns crestfallen to see my sister and me already tucking into our sandwiches.

"I thought your mother had put them in the boot?" he says.

"No, we've been keeping them company in here," says my sister pointing to the adjacent cardboard box with one hand whilst deftly passing an egg and cress sandwich through the window with the other.

We all munch on in contented silence as Dad goes about aligning the mugs on the Morris's bonnet before adeptly dispatching tea in each.

"At least it's stopped raining," my sister says as we sip our drinks. With that, a few drops of water appear on the windscreen.

"Oh, looks like I spoke too soon," she adds.

"Don't worry, it's only a bit of moisture from the tea," I reply, observing the flask, which still stands steaming on the bonnet like some ancient locomotives funnel.

Mum returns in a buoyant mood, obviously uplifted by her brief ecclesiastical experience.

Unfortunately, this change of mood is short-lived when she discovers we have eaten her egg and cress sandwiches.

She contents herself with the remaining cheese and pickle while Dad leans casually on the side of the car puffing at his pipe. Suitably refreshed, we are all back on board and underway once again.

Apart from a brief stop for nature outside the village

of Wingham, we are very soon closing in on our destination.

However, fairly soon after this, the atmosphere in the car becomes tense as we stop at a T-junction for several minutes while Mum and Dad debate on whether to go right or left.

After consulting the map Dad for once get his own way, but after a few miles, the road starts getting progressively narrower until, inevitably, we reach a farmyard entrance secured by a five-bar gate.

"Have we arrived?" I ask.

"Nice campsite," adds my sister with a hint of sarcasm.

These comments are somewhat unappreciated by Mum, who temporarily loses her temper, shouting at us both to shut up, firmly instructing Dad to turn the car round and go back to the previous junction.

With much effort, Dad attempts a three-point turn in a lane the same width as the Morris.

Successfully completing this tricky manoeuvre on about the eighteenth attempt, he emits a long audible sigh.

Misinterpreting his reactions for one of annoyance instead of the physical effort involved in hauling a heavily overloaded car through one hundred and eighty degrees, Mum unfairly starts berating him for taking the wrong turning.

Needless to say, by now, feelings in the car have become distinctly chilly.

We arrive at the now familiar junction once again and come to a juddering halt. Out comes the map once again.

"If we go straight on here, then take the next right," says Dad, illustrating his intentions on the map with the stem of his unlit pipe. "That should lead us back onto the main road."

We proceed straight ahead, take the next right and very soon arrive back at the same T-junction once more.

"Brilliant," says Mum, "What now?"

Gently bringing the car to a halt, Dad carefully takes the map from Mum's lap, slowly winds down the window, and flings it out onto the road.

My sister and I exchange incredulous looks. Simultaneously he calmly engages first gear, and we drive off in total silence.

For once, Mum is obviously too shocked to even open her mouth.

In fact, it's several minutes before anyone says anything. Finally, after what seems an age it's Dad who breaks the silence.

"It was a bloody rubbish map anyway," he says bluntly.

Nobody mourns the loss of our trusty road guide; in truth, its very existence had led to many an argument between my parents. Well done, Dad, for finally making a stand and taking action.

Mercifully, and not before one or two more wrong turns, we eventually see a sign displaying "Camp Site 100 yds Left," and very soon, we are gratefully rewarded with our first sight of *Plucks Gutter*.

THE CARROLLS GO CAMPING 3
(aka: In the Gutter)

It has to be said first impressions are not good.

Pulling into the pot-holed car park of *The Dog and Duck*, the pub adjacent to the campsite, the first sight that greets us is two or three semi-derelict caravans. These are pushed up close together, presumably to prevent them from toppling over

Dad pulls up beside a brick wall by several large Calor gas cylinders. "Well, looks like this is it," he says cheerfully.

We survey the bleak scene.

They have obviously recently had a heavy shower as the car park is a mass of large brown puddles, more of a worry though is the field in front of the pub which we understand to be the campsite.

Is it a field or a boating lake?

From where we sit, it resembles the latter.

Dad removes his glasses and gives them a polish with his handkerchief, puts them back on, and says, "That must be the camping field then. Good job we packed the wellingtons."

My sister and I look at Mum with apprehension, waiting for a reaction. We expect her to say something like, "Right, George, turn the car round. We are going home."

Untypical of her, though, she climbs out of the car and goes to the boot to fetch our wellingtons.

Dad turns in his seat, gives us an encouraging smile, and says, "Come on, this will be fun."

So, while Mum, my sister, and I get weather-equipped, Dad disappears around the back of the pub to look for the proprietor. His departure coincides with it starting to rain more heavily, resulting in the three of us having to get back in the car again.

As I peer out through the steamed-up windscreen at the bleak view, I can just discern the pub sign swinging back and forth in the wind.

Its jaunty cartoon image depicting a cheeky spaniel and his feathered friend totally at odds with the ambient view.

Several minutes tick by. My sister and I are amusing ourselves with games of noughts and crosses on the steamy windows.

"Don't know where your father got to," says Mum as the rain gets heavier with a bit of hail thrown in for good measure.

Eventually, after about twenty minutes, a ghostly figure emerges from the pub's front door and starts sprinting towards us. Wasting no time as the rain is now of monsoon proportion, Dad flings open the car door smartly, planting himself breathlessly into the driver's seat.

Indifferent to his sodden appearance Mum immediately questions why he has been so long. He's just in the process of explaining why when she remarks on the smell of beer in the car. My sister and I exchange knowing smirks.

"Well, the landlord was just on his own enjoying a quiet drink, and he kindly asked me if I would like to join him. I could hardly refuse now, could I?" he says openly.

"Well, thanks very much. While we're stuck in here watching it bucketing down, you're in the dry swilling beer. Honestly, George," she says.

"Sorry, dear," he says somewhat lamely before adding, "Apparently, they've got a family room at the back, which we're welcome to use while we wait for it to clear up."

Dad looks vainly out of the windows in the hope of a break in the rain and an escape from Mum's wrath.

"If I go round the back and get him to open the front door when you see me, you can make a run for it, what do you reckon," he says.

"Well, I'm definitely not prepared to sit in the car all day, George, so I suggest you get cracking," she says waspishly.

With that, he's off across the car park like a greyhound who just spotted the hare.

We all watch him disappear from view, keenly waiting for the front door to open. It seems like an eternity. Surely, he can't be having another drink, I think.

Eventually, after several minutes he appears, and without hesitation, we alight from the car, niftily sidestepping the large puddles en route to the door.

It's very dark and gloomy inside the pub, with an overpowering smell of stale beer and cigarettes pervading. Dad shepherds us through the main bar area down a narrow corridor and in through a brown door with the sign "Family Room" above.

At one end is a Victorian fireplace (unlit) with a shelf above, upon which sits a smokey overmantel mirror. In the middle of the room stands an ancient trestle table complemented by a rich assortment of chairs.

Apart from a very threadbare rug and a couple of dingy watercolours, there's little else of interest save for an old dart board that has clearly seen plenty of action. Most Police Station interview rooms would likely be more welcoming.

"Right," says Dad, "Make yourselves comfy, and I'll get us some drinks."

"Can I come with you?" asked my sister.

"No, your father will have to go on his own. Children aren't allowed through into the bar," says Mum.

Dad takes our orders, a shandy for Mum, ginger beer for me, and orange juice for my sister, plus three packets of crisps to help lift our spirits.

By the time he returns, I've discovered some darts on the shelf above the fireplace and my sister and I are doing our best to add some woodworm effects to the surrounding walls.

"I've been chatting to the landlord, and he assures me that the field drains very quickly," says Dad with an optimistic look, adding, "He says if we pitch our tents up against the fence close to the river at the top of the field it's pretty dry there."

He looks to Mum for some sign of encouragement. When none comes, he continues with, "Of course, we'll have to leave the car in the car park for now, or at least until it's dry enough to bring it up by the tents."

Mum, up to now, has remained unusually quiet,

slowly sipping her drink while casually observing our attempt at darts, periodically glancing outside to check on the weather.

"So then, dear, what you are suggesting is we are going to have to lug all the camping gear up the field? Brilliant."

"I'm afraid that's the strength of it, love," he says.

Little more is said on the subject while we munch on our crisps and finish our drinks. However, it's plain to see Mum is less than thrilled with this arrangement.

Fortunately, our gloomy mood is soon given a welcome boost with the sudden appearance of a shaft of sunlight permeating the room. This unexpected appearance only enhances the general shabbiness of our surroundings.

So, when Dad signals his customary clapping of his palms together with "Let's get cracking. It seems to be clearing up," it's no hardship to hastily make our way out of the pub into the dazzling sunshine.

Indeed, so intense is the light, comparable to leaving a cinema during the daytime, it takes us a while for our eyes to adjust to our new surroundings.

THE CARROLLS GO CAMPING 4

(aka Tales from the River Bank)

Once we become accustomed to the light and start to familiarise ourselves with our new environment, it becomes plainly evident that manually carrying all the camping gear up the field closer to the river would be a monumental job, even for a small army.

Dad surveys the task in hand and, in accordance with Mum, decides to attempt to drive the car around the perimeter where the ground looks firmer.

Wisely, he decides to remove some of the luggage from the boot first, to somewhat lighten the load.

He sets off across the car park in a business-like manner while we watch on with slight apprehension

I'm wondering what driving method he is going to adopt.

Will he take it gently in low gear? Or, as I am hoping, get some speed up across the car park first before launching the car at the field?

Dad doesn't disappoint. Settling for the latter approach, he blips the throttle, ala Formula One, before swinging the car around in a full circle and making for the edge of the field

The little Morris sounds quite purposeful and hunkered down on its springs has enhanced its new sporty character.

Progress initially is more than satisfactory, with half the distance up the field negated without drama. However, within a few more yards, things get a bit dramatic when the car starts to fishtail wildly before spinning through 180 degrees and finally slowing to a stop.

Dad attempts a few futile attempts to get going, but with so much mud now on the rear tyres, traction is totally lost.

The Morris clearly is here to stay for a while until the field dries out. My sister and I enthusiastically run up to join him

As he climbs out of the car, pipe clenched in his teeth, the flat cap on at a jaunty angle, he resembles an early racer.

"Well done, Dad, that was fantastic," I say, congratulating him on his driving prowess, adding, "You nearly made it."

Mum arrives and appears a trifle less impressed, suggesting a lower gear might have been better suited to the conditions.

Wisely, he chooses to ignore this remark, opting instead by beginning to untie the tents from the roof

I start to give him a hand while Mum and my sister commence unloading the remainder of the luggage from the boot.

It takes us several trips to transport all our gear to a suitable dry pitch in the top corner of the field close to the hedge. This spot dually provides a bit of shelter, also somewhere private if we happen to be taken short in the night. The only downside to our chosen spot is that the area, although dry, is far from level.

Now, if you happen to know anything about pitching a tent, the most important aspect is to try to find level ground.

Thus, it was that when we finally manage to erect our two tents, neither prove to be a comfortable place to spend much time in.

One of the tents will house my Mum and all the food, catering equipment, clothes, etc., while Dad, me and my sister will be in the other. Slightly unconventional sleeping arrangements, you might think, but I guess having an adult in each tent should prevent arguments between us all.

Frankly, I was more than a little disappointed with the tents. I had been hoping Dad had borrowed continental-style frame tents, which were beginning to prove very popular at that time. This was obviously wishful thinking. I should have realised when I saw they were housed in old hessian kit bags that we were in for something more rustic.

Fully erected, not a job for the faint-hearted, especially as we have to deal with a firm breeze, the finished article resembled something from a Boy Scout Jamboree.

Slightly embarrassed but relieved that we are the only ones in the field, we stand back to admire our work.

While Mum busies herself with organising the domestic arrangements and Dad pauses for a welcome smoke, my sister and I decide to do a bit of exploring. Charged by Mum that our first chore will be to locate the toilets, and secondly to find the standpipe, we set off with the Jerry can.

The first port of call will be the pub, where I guessed we would find some toilets. This proves correct, although the amenities turn out to be very basic indeed; the mens' just an aluminium trough plus a couple of cubicles, the ladies, according to my sister, just two cubicles. So, no washing facilities then.

My experience of our caravan holidays with wash basins, showers, and laundry rooms is a distant fond memory.

While waiting for my sister to report back her findings, I spot the standpipe sprouting from the outer wall of the block.

Although conveniently placed, it is positioned too

high on the wall to facilitate easy filling as one has to lift the Jerry can get up to the tap. This is clearly a two-man job, as the effort needed to just hold the can precludes the operation of the flow. The result is a half-full can and soaking wet shorts.

I'm glad I have had the sense to keep my wellingtons on.

Returning to the tents with our water, I find that Mum and Dad are in fits of laughter over their attempts to assemble the camp beds. Nice, I think to see them in such a jolly mood.

The beds would be a constant source of amusement during our holiday, none of us ever quite sure whether they would last the night without spontaneously collapsing on us.

Our domestic duties were completed, and my sister and I decided to go for a stroll to view the river.

This doesn't take very long as we are camped right next to it. However, to get to the other bank involves going back across the field towards the pub, out through the car park, and taking the road bridge. This takes us about ten minutes, and when we arrive opposite our pitch, we are in a position to give our parents a cheery wave. We stand for a while waving and shouting quite loudly, but after a minute with no response, we head off further along the bank.

"Must still be busy with those silly beds," says my sister.

"Maybe," I reply before adding, "Come on, I want to find the best place to do some fishing from."

The River Stour is quite wide, fast flowing, and tidal at this point, it's not very accessible either, but after a few hundred yards, the bank is much lower, offering several likely places to fish from.

We clamber down to inspect, careful not to slip on the muddy slope. Safely down to river level, we both stare vacantly at the dark, murky water.

"Looks awfully deep," my sister proclaims.

"Very," I reply. "We need to be careful.

Having satisfied my angling expectations, we spend the next half hour or so happily playing "Poo Sticks" with bits of dead reed.

"I think we should be getting back. They must have got those beds up by now," says my sister.

I nod in agreement, and we cautiously navigate our way up the bank onto the towpath.

THE CARROLLS GO CAMPING 5
(aka On the Beach)

Back at the camp, Mum and Dad are still in a jolly mood.

They seem to have satisfactorily erected the camp beds and have them stowed neatly in their respective tents.

Mum is preparing a meal while Dad fiddles with the Calor gas stove.

The sun is still shining brightly, and the weather looks set fair, in sharp contrast to earlier in the day.

The field, as predicted by the Landlord, has drained well, and our beached Morris apart, the scene is one of peaceful tranquility.

Later, after being suitably fed and watered, we all take a stroll along the riverbank. I point out the likely fishing spot to Mum, and we both decide to give it a go in the morning. I have only recently introduced her to fishing and having given her my old rod, and some tackle she's become really enthusiastic.

In fact, I'll freely admit that she's much more interested than me.

She appears to enjoy the peace and calm of sitting for

hours watching a float, whereas I end up getting a bit bored after about twenty minutes.

Returning suitably relaxed to our homely little settlement, we arrange our chairs outside the tents to fully appreciate the fiery sunset of reds and oranges as the sun slowly dips over the edge of the field.

"Time to call it a day, me thinks," says Dad stifling a yawn.

With no bathroom facilities available on the site, it takes quite a time to attend to our needs, each taking our turn with the washing-up bowl, keeping Dad active with having to constantly boil kettles.

Unsurprisingly, my sister and I are not too fussy about this activity. However, Mum is insistent hygiene standards are maintained.

Having reluctantly complied with her wishes, we are ready to experience our first night under canvas.

Mum eagerly escapes to the sanctuary of her single occupancy.

At least it will guarantee her some peace and quiet, with the added benefit of being able to help herself to a snack at night if she gets peckish.

Dad, I guess, has drawn the short straw as he's condemned to sharing with my sister and I.

Our beds are positioned three abreast, with Dad in between us to ensure we behave. This doesn't, however, preclude us from giggling and talking rubbish for ages before, eventually, we succumb to sleep.

I wake several times during the night. On each occasion experiencing the unpleasant notion I'm performing a sort of back flip.

This weird feeling I transpire is due to my camp bed facing uphill. Something I need to rectify in the morning.

Nothing seems to have disturbed the other two, who judging by their perpetual snoring, seem totally oblivious of the problem.

Ultimately, after a fitful night's sleep, dawn eventually arrives. I tentatively roll up the side curtain to inspect the day.

Although the view from ground level is somewhat limited, it at least gives me the opportunity to run my hand across the grass, experiencing the freshness of the heavy dew.

I'm also aware of the stillness, no noise either, save for the distant sound of some sheep in a far-off field.

I turn back to face Dad, observing his gentle breathing and the comforting tobacco-fuelled aroma he emits.

My relaxed state is soon interrupted by my sister, who asks if I am awake.

When I reply with a "No," she informs me that she's already observed me peeping out under the canvas.

This brief conversation is enough to disturb Dad, who enquires as to our night's sleep.

I explain my strange night-time experience, proceeding to inform him that we need to try and find somewhere more level to pitch the tent.

Resolving to give it a try, he slowly sits up and stretches while absently feeling under the covers for his pipe. Although a habitual smoker, I've noticed he rarely lights it straight away in the morning but is just satisfied to use it as a kind of pacifier. Very endearing.

Smoking apparatus firmly in place, he climbs out of his sleeping bag, unties the tent flap, and departs to get the kettle on for our early morning cuppa.

While he's busy with the stove, my sister and I share our plans for the day. She wants to go to the beach while I am happy to stay here and try a spot of fishing.

In the end, to avoid any argument, we agree to let our parents decide.

While my sister goes to lobby Dad. I get up to go and lend Mum a hand with the breakfast.

I'm entrusted with erecting the picnic table, a vicious piece of equipment I'm all too familiar with. I take ultra-care in this task, having previously experienced trapped fingers in its awkward hinges.

Job painlessly completed, I don my wellies and trudge off over the damp field to the toilets. I Pass the stranded Morris, which appears to have sunk further into the mud overnight. I give the bonnet an affectionate tap, whispering assurances that we'll come and rescue it soon.

My ablutions satisfactorily carried out, crossing the field, I hear the shrill sound of the kettle as I approach the tents.

"Tea's ready," says Dad, passing me a mug

"Weather looks fine for a trip to the beach," he says.

"Assuming we can get the car unstuck," I reply.

"Should be able to move it ok now. The fields have dried out a lot since yesterday. You can give me a hand after breakfast if you like."

"Will we have time for a fish later then?" I enquire.

"Don't see why not. We won't be there all day; we have to please your sister sometimes, old lad."

"Looks like you got your own way with the beach then,"

I say to my sister as she emerges from the tent with the breakfast plates. She treats me to a little knowing smile as she arranges them on the picnic table. I'm all too aware of Dad being putty in her hands.

After breakfast, Dad and I make our way across the field to the car. He decides straight away it might be an idea to put the rubber floor mats under the rear wheels to improve traction.

This task complete, Dad climbs in, starts the engine, selects first gear, and eases out the clutch. The rear tyres grip, and the little car begins to climb out of the rut.

But just when I think it's nearly out, the wheels start spinning again, and frustratingly it drops back. He tries a few more times but still gets the same result.

He stops the engine, climbs out, and comes round to have a look. "Mmm," he mutters, "What we need is someone to give us a bit of a push."

No sooner have the words left his lips than we spot two men with fishing gear making their way toward us.

"Need a shove, mate?" says one.

"We'll soon get you going," says the other.

With all three of us pushing and Dad giving it plenty of revs, the car catapults out of its slushy furrow, showering us in a mixture of mud and grass.

The two fishermen being suitable attired don't fair too badly. I, on the other hand, get splattered from head to foot in soggy clods of brown soil.

Both men look at me and start laughing.

"Well, looks like you've copped the lot, son," says one to the other.

As I slowly squelch back to the tent, I can still hear them laughing from the far side of the field.

My sister can barely contain her amusement either, and even Mum manages a smile, tempered somewhat with thoughts of how she is going to wash out my clothes.

"I shouldn't bother about getting cleaned up, lad we're off to the seaside in a bit. You can get a good wash there," he says jokingly while engaged in wiping the mud from the Morris's windscreen.

Hearing his good-natured gibe, Mum sympathetically adds. "Leave it to dry, dear. Most of it will brush off."

Feeling slightly dejected, I seek out the washing-up bowl, fill it with cold water and attempt to make myself presentable.

Having cleaned up as best I could, I proceed to help Dad load the car with the beach gear.

Fortunately, the day is turning out warm, with the sun shining brightly in a clear blue sky. So, with luck, I'll soon be able to get out of these soiled garments and into my swimming trunks.

Once ready and all seated in the car, Mum inquires as to where we are going. Dad is just in the throes of asking her to consult the map when he remembers and abruptly stops mid-sentence.

"Precisely," she says

"We'll have to wing it," he adds smartly, selecting first gear, tentatively navigating a safe, dry route around the field, out across the car park, and onto the main road.

Fortunately for him and more by luck than good fortune, he manages to find the sea without too many diversions.

Satisfactorily parked close to the beach, we trudge down the pebbles with all our beach paraphernalia.

Not wishing to go through the usual complicated rigmarole of changing into my trunks on the beach, I've taken the opportunity to carry out a nifty manoeuvre in transit. This delicate operation is amusingly observed by my sister, who naturally has had the forethought to get her costume on beforehand.

Finding a convenient spot on the sparsely populated beach isn't a problem, so once settled, I quickly disrobe and rush off to meet the ocean.

Despite the warm August day, the water is still surprisingly cold. Consequently, my eagerness to get finally free of my mud-caked appearance is swiftly arrested.

This doesn't, however, deter Dad, who true to form launches himself at the waves, rapidly proceeding like a human torpedo in the direction of Calais.

I tentatively take a few more steps, and before totally committing myself to my quest, I turn to observe Mum and my sister sitting comfortably afar, eagerly watching my deliberations.

Accordingly, I make a snap decision and, so as not to disappoint them, I try emulating a similar entry to Dad.

This proves a big mistake, as one, I have grossly underestimated the cold, and two, the steep shelf of the shingle seabed I have been safely perched on.

Needless to say, after several panic-fuelled seconds in which I feel I might be drowning, I thankfully emerge safe on the surface, having suffered nothing worse than a few mouthfuls of the English Channel.

I scope the shore to check on their reactions to my near-death experience, only to see that they have vacated their spot and are now occupying a place in the queue for ice cream.

"Great, well, I hope they're getting one for me."

Having needlessly put my life at risk in the cause of cheap entertainment, I waste no time washing off the dried mud.

For no one's benefit save my own, I try a couple of feeble attempts at breaststroke before calling it a day, finally wading cheerlessly out of the water and stumbling up the beach to join them in the queue.

"Did you see me nearly drowning?" I say to them.

"We thought you were just messing about," says Mum.

Although slightly staggered at their lack of concern, I decide it's probably not worth pursuing the conversation as they seem more interested in their choice of ice cream. Earnestly discussing the merits of the new 99 cone as opposed to the traditional wafer.

A short while later, and with Dad having returned from his mammoth swim, we all sit gazing at the ocean while contentedly licking our ice creams.

"Can we go fishing when we get back?" I tentatively enquire.

"Thought you might have had enough water for one day," says Dad with a chuckle.

"First a mud bath, then he nearly drowns; you think it's safe for him to go fishing?" my sister chimes in.

They all look at me for a response. But when none comes, Dad says, "We'll see."

The remainder of the day passes in peaceful family harmony, enjoying a picnic, followed by an energetic game of beach rounders. We eventually, sated by the sun and pleasantly tired, decide it's time to make our way back to camp.

THE CARROLLS GO CAMPING 6

(aka A Brief Slice of Entente Cordiale)

Back at "the Gutter," as we now affectionately refer to it, Dad and I set about repositioning our tent on level ground. This is not a simple task as the field is far from flat, resembling more of an overgrown meadow than a proper campsite.

We do our best, but standing back to inspect our handiwork, it's clearly evident the tent now appears to be listing to one side.

"Reckon that's the best we can do," he says, hands on hips. "Time for a cuppa, I think."

I don't agree, but I can't expect him to move it again, so reluctantly, I start stowing everything back inside while he ambles off to fill the kettle.

After our exertion with the tent, fetching water, cooking a meal, washing up, and all the hundred or so jobs that camping seems to throw up, dusk has arrived, and it's nearly time for bed.

Aware of my disappointment at not getting any fishing in today, Mum suggests we can make an early start tomorrow before breakfast. This seems appealing, and with that, I readily set about preparing for bed, eagerly expectant of a good night's sleep.

Washed and pyjama'd, I am the first in the tent. Importantly I spend some time re-attaching the legs on the camp bed, bouncing on it a few times to ensure it will take my weight without collapsing. Next, I check to see if I have my torch close at hand in case I need to leave the tent for a wee before finally climbing in and zipping up my sleeping bag.

My sister arrives shortly and deploys a similar routine. Satisfied, she carefully arranges her array of soft toys in their sleeping positions before snuggling down to join them.

Looking across and observing her actions, it's plainly obvious that her bed is significantly higher than mine.

"Hello down there," she says, stifling a giggle.

"Don't know what you're laughing at, you'll probably be joining me later. I think we're all going to end up in this corner!" I say.

The tent flap suddenly parts, and in stumbles Dad. "All good, kids?" he says breezily.

"Yes, we're fine," we answer in unison.

Dad wastes no time in preparing his bed before

bidding us a quick "Good night, sleep tight," and within minutes, he's snoring his head off.

Sleep escapes me. The adventures of the day conspiring to deny me.

I turn over very carefully so as not to disturb the fragile camp bed from giving way.

I am now facing the outer wall of the tent and have found a more comfortable position.

Satisfied, I soon start to drift off.

I am just entering that blissful point of unconsciousness when suddenly I am aware of a bright light sweeping through the canvas. This is instantly accompanied by the sound of a car engine.

Not a recognisable one by its uneven beat.

If I don't mind saying myself, I'm a bit of a nerd when it comes to cars, and this one is so unfamiliar it has me totally foxed.

My senses are now fully switched on as I lie on my side, fully alert.

Up to now, we have had the campsite completely to ourselves, so I guess it should be no surprise that sooner or later we would get some neighbours.

After running for a few more minutes, the engine

is switched off, allowing me to detect some far-off conversation.

Again, this is unfamiliar. Could I be dreaming? It's definitely not English voices I can hear in the field.

Maybe German? No, not German, French then. Yes, French, not that I can hear much of it as they are obviously some distance away.

I can detect several voices, both male and female.

I'm intrigued, so gently, so as not to disturb the other two, I carefully lifted the edge of the canvas, removing one of the tent pegs and allowing me to raise it just sufficiently to see what was going on.

The moon has conveniently come up, so I am able to clearly make out several figures busily extracting luggage from the vehicle. There seem to be four of them, two adults and two children.

I watch intently as they arrange stuff on the grass in a highly organised way.

They give the impression of experienced campers as they all seem to have a designated job to do. There is a certain admirable organised look to their endeavours. Maybe they're German after all.

Within minutes they have the canvas laid out on the ground and have constructed a tubular frame. Seconds later, this has been placed over the frame, and the whole tent raised up into habitable living accommodation. Incredible.

In the time it would have taken us to extract our tents from the hessian bags and sort out all numerous poles and guy- ropes, they have constructed a modern living space.

Not just any space, either. This is one an adult could walk into without having to make a "Quasimodo" impression.

I watch for a little longer before deciding I must get some sleep.

Drifting off, I wonder who they are and speculate what they might make of our primitive camping equipment in the cold light of day.

My dreams of attempting to erect a tent in a sea of mud are Interrupted by a rustling of the canvas.

Sitting up and rubbing sleep from my eyes, I focus on a spectral hand untying the flap, swiftly followed by Mum's face.

"Are you ready then?" she whispers.

Quietly, so as not to disturb the others, I slide forward out of my cocoon and emerge gingerly from the tent.

"You'll probably going to need a jacket as it's a bit chilly," she says in a hushed voice.

I decamp to her tent to get dressed, choosing to leave my pyjamas on underneath as an extra precaution against the cold.

Suitably kitted out with all our fishing gear, we make our way across the field.

"Looks like we've got company. Best keep our voices down until we get over the other side of the bridge," she whispers.

There's no sign of life as we skirt past their tent. I take note of its neat modern appearance together with the odd-looking vehicle parked alongside it.

Mum asks, "That's a very strange-looking car. What is it?"

"I think it's a Panhard p17, two cylinders, air cooled engined," I reply knowledgeably.

"Never seen one before, but thought you would know," she says with a smile.

We cross the bridge and make our way down the towpath in the direction of the spot I had earmarked.

To our surprise and disappointment, it's already occupied, so we continue on for several hundred yards until we come to a small bridge where the river divides. Choosing to stay on the same side, we walk on a little further.

We are just at the point of giving up and retracing our steps when we come across a perfect place where the bank is not too steep, allowing easy access down to the river.

We climb down and start setting up our equipment.

Neither of us is proficient in the art of angling, and with a fast-flowing tidal river, we lack the experience and knowledge to make the best of the conditions.

Firstly, there's the need to frequently wind the line in to recast, and secondly, as we only have bread paste for bait, it's constantly falling off our hooks.

Mum, as I have said, has more patience than me. Consequently, after about an hour, I've lost interest and keen to call it a day and head back for breakfast.

She isn't fazed when I say I'm going back; in truth, I think she's more than happy to be left on her own.

Making my way back down the towpath, I notice our first choice spot is now vacant, and when I approach the bridge,

I see the fisherman packing his rods into an old van. "Morning," he says cheerfully, "No luck then?"

"No," I reply.

"Left 'yer Mum to it, 'ave you?" he continues.

"Yes, I think she prefers to be on her own."

"Won't catch nothing now till the tide turns, bout eleven, I'd say," he adds.

"Really, oh, thanks. I'll bear that in mind then."

"No problem," he says, climbing into his van, "Have a good day."

He gives me a final respectful touch of his cap, releases the handbrake, and with a grinding whine of its aged starter followed by painful mashing of gears, the van disappears across the bridge in a cloud of dust.

Returning to the campsite, Dad is already up and about.

He has his shaving mirror perched on top of the Morris's roof, and with a brush in hand, he gesticulates towards the camping table, indicating a mug of tea already poured out for me.

"Saw you coming over the bridge," he says.

"Where's your mother? I hope you haven't drowned her," he adds with a chuckle.

"Didn't catch anything then," says my sister.

"No, I think we got the tide all wrong or something, according to some old fisherman I've just been chatting with," I reply.

"The Tale of the Ancient Mariner," chips in Dad whilst absently wiping the remaining soap from his chin with a tea towel.

"Just as well Mum's not here to see you doing that," says my sister teasing him.

"See we've got some neighbours then, must have arrived late last night," she adds

"Think they could be French, or maybe they just like to drive foreign cars, judging by that strange choice of vehicle," says Dad.

"What about their tent Dad, don't you think it's neat?"

"One puff of wind it'll collapse like a pack of cards. You can't beat good old British Army Ridge Tents, son," swiftly adding, "I'll have you know these tents here…" breaking off to gesticulate with his pipe, "Provided first-class shelter across several continents, in all weathers, for millions of our boys, right through two World Wars."

I was about to dispute this when out of the corner of my eye, I catch sight of movement from the very object of our conversation

Exiting the tent is a girl of similar age to myself, I guess.

Slowly sipping my tea, I keenly follow her progress down the field. She cuts an attractive figure, swinging two large Jerry cans in a carefree manner, blissfully unaware of her impending baptism with the intricacies of the campsites standpipe.

My sister, following my gaze, says with slight bitchy intent, "She's in for a nice surprise. I hope she's got a dry set of clothes."

Dad forgetting his army, reminiscing for a moment, and having observed my interest, suggests it might be prudent for me to go and give her a hand

Needing no further prompting, I set off in leisurely pursuit.

Reaching the corner of the field, I pause by the fence at the rear of the pub, allowing me the opportunity of taking a peek through the slats to check on her progress.

She stands side on to me, one hand resting on her hip, the other intently fiddling with the tap. Next, she's leaning forward, brushing her hair behind her ears to make a closer inspection. Don't they have taps in France?

As she attempts to fathom the intricacies of the British water system, I continue to observe her.

Typical of most thirteen-year-old boys, I lack experience when it comes to dealing with the opposite sex. True, I have a sister, but I don't think that counts much in my favour.

My opinion of girls up to now has been that they are either moaning, giggling about something, or generally being a pain in the butt. Also, they are pretty hopeless at sports.

Recently, however, I can see they might be of some use.

This one, however, appears a bit different, or to phrase it more appropriately, she exudes a certain "je ne sais quoi."

My adolescent study of the female form is unfortunately short-lived as suddenly she has gone from scrutinising the tap to flaying it with one of her sandals.

Time I think, for me to make my "knight in shining armour" appearance. Straightening my jacket and smoothing my hair back, I attempt a casual approach from behind the fence.

I cough discreetly to attract her attention. This doesn't work as she continues her assault on the tap.

I revert to the common language, praying she understands some English.

"Excuse me," I begin. "Do you want some help with the tap?"

"Pardon?" she replies.

"I said, can I give you a hand?" much louder this time to avoid repeating myself.

"Dis does not work?"

"Yes."

Could be in a bit of trouble here, I'm thinking.

"No, it works fine. You have to push down on it. Can I show you?"

"S'il te plait S'il vous plait" she replies.

Seeing my gormless expression causes her to smile, and suppressing a laugh, she says, "Oui, I think that would 'elp."

Privately, thanking the gods that she speaks some English, I pick up one of the Jerry cans and proceed to demonstrate how to operate the tap.

This goes well until the cans are half-full, suddenly becoming too heavy and no longer in control. My muscles urge me to put it down.

Noticing my dilemma, she quickly comes to my assistance. This has both positive and negative results.

While her helping me hold the can up to the tap relieves my muscles, her close proximity is affecting my senses, and before I realise it, the water is overflowing the spout sending a gushing spray of water into our faces.

She lets out a little scream.

"Sacre bleu, b******s," I reply.

We both stand upright and inspect each other. Smiling broadly and pointing to my jacket, she says, "You are very wet."

"You've not done too badly yourself," I add.

Noticing her own wet t-shirt, she cries out, "Oh, Mon Dieu."

Quickly, I gallantly go about removing my damp jacket to curtail her embarrassment. Passing it to her, she carefully inspects it, nods her acceptance, and with a brief Gallic shrug, puts it on. Satisfied, she then completes the performance with an enchanting toss of her hair, a three hundred and sixty-degree turn finally culminating with a provocative pout of her lips.

I give her my wide-mouth frog impression. We both fall into fits of laughter.

Hers turning to screams when she notices my Rupert Bear pyjamas.

Now, it's my turn to be embarrassed.

"Ow, very sweet," she says, nearly collapsing.

"Thank you," I replied, blushing, adding a feeble, "Christmas present from my mother."

After we have both calmed down a bit and she has her giggles under control, I suggest we try to fill the other can.

Proceeding this time with more caution, I keep a steady eye on the level, ensuring there's no repeat performance.

Task accomplished, she's first with the introductions.

"Qui est votre nom?" she says before apologising and quickly reverting to English.

"What is your name?"

"O, um, I'm Richard," I reply.

"Pascale," she says, formally offering me her hand

Introductions over, I suggest we better be getting back, just remembering I still hadn't had any breakfast.

As we make our way across the field, she suddenly stops and turns to face me. "You know you are very good, Boy Scout. I think you 'ave, 'ow you say, done your duty, yes?"

"Sorry?" I reply, somewhat confused.

"You are Boy Scout, yes?"

Still baffled, I offer, "Well, I was in the cubs" "What is 'cubs,' please?"

I am just about to explain this when she says, "You live in Scout tents, yes?" The penny drops.

Those ****** tents…

"Actually, Pascale," I say, pleased with being able to use her name for the first time, "We only use them for camping. Our proper home is a bungalow."

Now it's her turn to look confused. "What is a bungalow?" she asks sweetly.

"Well, it's a small house with…" Fortunately, my

limited architectural knowledge remains un-stretched as her father is calling her from their tent.

"He is wanting is water. I 'ave to go," she says, breaking into a run.

I'm impressed with her athleticism; even with a half-full jerry can, she streaks ahead of me.

I arrive panting a good thirty seconds later, to be greeted by her father, who welcomes me with a garlic-fuelled embrace and a slap on the back.

Pascale then says something to him, resulting in another emotional reaction. Fortunately, this time, he just gives me a big smile and ruffles my hair.

"I told 'im you are not a Boy Scout, but just a good cub. He says you are good to help a damsel in distress, yes?"

"Well, I did my best," I reply sheepishly.

The brief awkward silence is interrupted by my sister shouting across the field. "Mum says if you don't hurry up, you'll miss out on breakfast."

"You better go, or you will be hungry," says Pascale.

"Right, yes, I'll be on my way then," I say, adding, hopefully, "I'll see you later."

"Hopefully, yes," she replies.

Making my way across to our tents, I can hardly feel my feet touching the ground, and I don't think that has anything to do with not having to drag heavy water cans around.

THE CARROLLS GO CAMPING 7
(aka French Cricket)

Approaching our tents, I see my family sitting at the camping table, having breakfast.

My mother immediately inquires as to what I have done with my jacket.

Before I get a chance to explain, my sister, looking up from her cereal bowl, chips in with, "I saw that girl wearing it as she went back to her tent," pointing with her spoon in the general direction of their tent.

"Is that so? Why did you lend her your jacket, dear?" says Mum.

Sensing an imminent interrogation, Dad comes to my rescue with, "Well, she probably just felt a bit chilly, I expect," rubbing his shoulders to emphasise the point.

"That's right," I add, nodding in agreement.

"Well, see that she returns it. I only bought it for you last autumn. It's a very good jacket."

I can sense this is not the end of the enquiry. Nevertheless, satisfied, for now, Mum continues with her breakfast.

Dad gives me a wink and changes the subject.

"I take it you didn't catch anything then?" he asks Mum.

"No, George, but you know it was lovely out there this morning, so peaceful just watching the wildlife. Absolute heaven."

It's been decided in my absence that we are going off on a trip to the local village of Wingham this morning.

Mum insists we need to buy some food, and Dad wants to check out a nearby camping shop that sells Calor Gas.

The camping shop turns out to be quite interesting, and while Dad is off busying himself with gas bottles, I get the chance to check out the equipment on offer. They have erected several models of the new continental frame tents and have them cleverly exhibited on a faux campsite. Climbing over the little plastic picket fence.

I take a peek inside.

Each tent has a zipped division separating the sleeping quarters from the cooking area. Fancy inflatable beds adorn the former while the latter display the latest cooking equipment. They even have a chemical toilet in its own little curtained-off section.

It all looks very inviting, a far cry from our dismal array of second-hand army surplus rejects.

I try to encourage Dad to look around but he's more concerned about returning to the car we have illegally parked on a yellow line in the High Street

Returning to the car, Mum is in a heated conversation with a traffic warden who is in the throes of writing us a ticket.

My sister and I scurry onboard while Dad stows the gas bottle in the boot.

She seems to be winning her case as the man is slowly putting his book back in his top pocket.

Mum can be quite a formidable opponent when she's in this mood, and I am genuinely starting to feel sorry for the poor fellow.

In fact, as Dad climbs in, I notice the warden is now quickly walking away, anxious to escape a tongue lashing.

Mum gets into the car and immediately transfers her wrath onto Dad for taking too long in the camping shop.

I am about to indulge her with details of the super new tents but wisely, in view of the frosty atmosphere in the car, I decide it's probably sensible to keep quiet.

Back at the campsite, I'm delighted to see my newfound French friends are still at home. Although there's no actual physical signs of them, their car is still parked by their tent, so I'm guessing they must be around somewhere.

After a hearty lunch of Mulligatawny soup followed by a spam salad with tinned fruit and carnation to finish, we are all in a slightly better mood.

While Mum goes for a lay down in her tent, I manage to coax Dad into a game of cricket. I'm thinking he, too, would prefer to have a little snooze, but like a good father, he agrees to a game.

My sister abstains as she's currently occupied with her newfound friend: a black and white cat, who, at the moment, she is trying to encourage (without success) to eat her leftover spam salad

We set off to find a level piece of ground to serve as a pitch.

This is not an easy task, as the field, although now quite dry, is far from ideal for cricket.

The best we can find is a bare patch of grass without too many humps and bumps, close to the fence. The downside of this location precludes playing any aerial shots, as these are likely to end up in the river.

Using a picnic chair as the wicket, I mark out the pitch, deciding that about twenty paces should be about righ

I let Dad bat first as I see myself as more of a bowler these days. Eager to experiment with some spin bowling but bearing in mind the pitch, I opt for a gentle medium pace.

The first few deliveries produce a wild variety of results. The ball skews off the ground in all directions, making it very tricky for the batsman to make a connection.

Dad suggests I should pitch it up a bit and try to bowl it fuller.

My first couple of efforts are too high, flying right over his head before colliding with the fence, which does a good job as our static wicketkeeper. Finally, I manage to get one on target, and Dad, unable to resist a straight ball, smashes it like a tracer bullet way over my head.

He holds his pose, clearly pleased with his effort.

Sadly, this stance is short-lived as we watch in horror at the ball's inevitable trajectory, straight towards our neighbour's tent.

Possibly worse than striking the canvas, which at least would have had some give, it crashes down on the bonnet of their car with a resounding clang.

Time stands still as we await to see if anyone emerges from the tent.

We don't have to wait long as the sound of the canvas zip is closely followed by Pascale's father.

Dressed only in a pair of pale blue underpants it's

clear we have probably disturbed his afternoon siesta.

Simultaneously scratching his head and yawning, he slowly scans the field for signs of what could have caused this sudden interruption to his forty winks.

I spot Dad surreptitiously attempting to hide the bat behind his back as I hold my breath, expecting some sort of confrontation.

Instead, what follows is surprising, to say the least.

Our French friend smiles warmly, gives us a friendly wave, and before returning to his tent, picks up our ball, skilfully demonstrating a useful overarm throw back to us.

Dad gives a shrug of his shoulders, returning to take up his position and await my next ball.

I'm just into my delivery stride when he holds up his hand, pointing in the direction of their tent.

Following his gaze, I see our friend emerging once again, this time fully dressed. He makes his way towards us, smiling broadly, and very soon, Dad, on this occasion, is the recipient of the garlic-fuelled embrace.

Through a series of comical mimes coupled with poor attempts at English and French translation, we learn his name is also George.

He indicates he is keen to join us for a game, and with my sister temporarily abandoning the cat, we now have some fielders.

As we all take our turn with bat and ball, it's evident that George (the French one, that is) is more than a bit handy, showing impressive cricketing skills for someone who comes from a country unfamiliar with the sport.

I am just about to bowl a ball to my sister, who has yet to connect with anything, despite me dollying them up from three yards, when my concentration is suddenly broken by the arrival of Pascale.

Despite her appropriate choice of the colour white, her inappropriate choice of tight shorts and matching top is at best alluring, at worst a terrible distraction.

Not waiting to be asked to join in, she quickly takes up a position close to my sister, who gives her a slightly haughty look.

I bowl the ball; my sister misses again.

Pascale retrieves the ball, treats me to a captivating smile, and moves in a little closer.

I bowl again, the same result, this time though my sister deliberately exaggerates her follow-through, narrowly missing Pascale's legs.

I sense an accident, intentional or otherwise, so signal Pascale to retreat a few steps.

The very next ball she finally connects with, sending it high in the air over the fence and into the river.

Pascale and I swiftly hop over the fence, but too late to retrieve the ball, which is already mid-stream and disappearing at a rate of knots on the outgoing tide.

She turns to me with a little frown. "Your sister, she is jealous, yes?" Surprised at the speed of her perception, I reply with, "No, of course not. She doesn't even know you."

Climbing back over the fence, she fixes me a look that implies I have plenty to learn about feminine instinct.

We return to the rest of the group who all look up in the hope of a successful outcome.

"I zinc we 'ave another ball," says Pascale, who runs across to fetch it from their tent.

"Where's she going?" enquires my sister.

"Fetching another ball," I reply.

"Was that a six?" she says with a hopeful look.

"Six and out, I'm afraid," I reply.

What follows is a prolonged and heated exchange of views between the two of us, in which I explain the rules of lost balls and forfeits.

My sister adamantly refuses to accept the decision,

angrily throwing the bat on the ground before stomping off towards our tent.

Unfortunately, this display of childish antics is witnessed by the addition of Pascale's brother, who has come to join in the game.

"Richard, go call her back," says Pascale in a surprising show of sisterly support. I call after her, but she chooses to ignore me. I reflect that I will probably pay for this later.

Pascale's introduces her brother Louis who is eight and, although lacking coordination with bat and ball, shares all of his sister's athleticism—valiantly running to all corners of the field, tirelessly retrieving everyone else shots, never complaining when he's out, and respectfully allowing others their turn.

We carry on having fun until Pascale's Mum calls them in for a meal.

Dad comes over, puts his arm across my shoulder, and says, "Well, that was a real pleasure, what a nice family," adding, "I've always maintained the frogs were a good bunch."

THE CARROLLS GO CAMPING 8
(aka The Dog & Duck & Cat)

Back at the tent, my sister has forgotten about our little disagreement and is eager to demonstrate her innovative method of dealing with our wasp problem.

Since arriving, these pesky insects have been plaguing us, especially annoying at mealtimes.

She has dug a small hole in the grass and scooped in some marmalade. The wasps find this irresistible, landing and gorging themselves, completely oblivious that they are about to be swiftly dispatched with the tent mallet.

With nothing else to do until tea time, we spend the next half hour or so actively reducing the local wasp population.

Maybe not ecologically sound, it does the trick, allowing us to enjoy our food undisturbed.

Teatime over, Dad suggests we might go over to the pub for an evening drink. This is enthusiastically received by my sister and me as a special treat.

In the event of us appearing like we are a bunch of gypsies, Mum insists we put on our best outfits.

As we are already over halfway through our holiday, this means our least dirty items, as most of us have already used up our quota of fresh clothes.

So, clean and shiny and suitably attired, we make our way over to the pub.

Not wishing to revisit the dubious delights of the "Family Room" once again, and as the evening is still warm, Dad suggests we can all sit outside.

The landlord has conveniently arranged a couple of metal tables and chairs just outside the door to the main bar, so it's around one of these that Mum, my sister, and I sit, eagerly awaiting Dad's return with the drinks.

Mum, I see, has done her best, with a smudge of lipstick and possibly a splash of eau de cologne, if I'm not mistaken. She's also found some stockings.

However, despite her neat appearance, she still looks a little tense, constantly fiddling with her wristwatch, coupled with frequent glances towards the pub door.

"I hope your father's not having another quick drink with the Landlord," she says rather tersely.

"I hope he isn't either, as just now everyone is getting on well. We don't want another scene."

Fortunately, he must have been reading my thoughts as

seconds later, he appears, carrying our tray of drinks.

Carefully placing the tray on the table, he sets about dispensing our refreshments. Mum has chosen a lager and lime, Dad a light ale, my sister a fizzy lemonade with a straw, and me all grown up with a shandy. He's also really pushed the boat out with four packets of crisps, two salt and vinegar, the other two the latest cheese and onion flavour.

My sister and I hastily snap up the cheese and onion, and we all eagerly tuck in. I'm still not sure if I like this camping lark, but just at this moment, the good weather, coupled with the relative harmony in the camp, has contrived to put me in good spirits.

My spirits improve even more when I catch sight of Pascale and her family making their way toward us.

She and her mother are resplendent in matching dark blue sun dresses. These are attractively decorated with white polka dots. She's also donned a pair of sunglasses perched strategically on her head, giving her the appearance of a French film star.

Pascale, however, is far from being overshadowed by her. By simply pulling her hair up into a chignon and applying a little makeup, she could well pass for her mother's younger sister.

Her father and brother are also not to be outdone by the ladies, wearing smart dark blue blazers with cream trousers.

They really look like the perfect Hollywood family.

I briefly glance across the table, observing my family's distinct lack of sartorial elegance.

Arriving at our table, Pascale, as the only member of her family with any English, proceeds to make the introductions.

There follows a highly awkward few moments as her family attempt the traditional French greeting of planting two kisses on each of our respective cheeks.

Thereby, after lots of banging of noses and "Pardons," they seat themselves down at the next table.

Dad immediately jumps to attention and enquires as to what they would like to drink.

Pascale begins translating, this bringing about several minutes of frantic discussion as to who wants what. Eventually, when all seems finally decided, she proceeds to dictate the order.

Mum, in anticipation and well-organised as ever, passes a pen and piece of paper torn from her diary for Dad to take the order.

Removing his glasses to concentrate on the task at hand, I spot a lovely red lipstick mark on his nose.

I point this out to my sister, who immediately starts giggling, the others quickly spot the joke, and soon we are all laughing gaily at poor old Dad.

"What?" he says, looking up from his notes, suddenly

acutely aware he has become the centre of attention. Mum whispers in his ear and passes him a hanky which he refuses, saying boldly. "I'll wear it as a badge of honour."

Pascale duly translates, and we all start laughing again

Well, Dad's certainly broken the ice; let's just hope he gets the drinks order right.

Pascale's dad offers to go with him, and the two Georges disappear through the pub door into the gloom of the bar.

While we wait patiently for our drinks, the little black and white cat befriended by my sister makes an appearance.

The women seem captivated, stroking and petting the animal who laps up the attention.

My sister passes some crisps to Pascale's brother Louis who attempts to encourage the cat to try one. The cat, in true feline manner, just sniffs it before suddenly jumping up on Pascale's mother's lap.

This brings about a shrill scream, followed by some French oath that needs no translation.

She jumps up and starts frantically brushing her dress, the cat, surprised by this sudden movement, takes flight across the table, in the process knocking my half-full glass of shandy all over my trousers

Great, I seem to be perpetually getting either soaking

wet covered in mud or, as now, drenched in shandy.

The girls find this highly amusing, but Pascale's mother exclaims, "Toi pauvre garcon!" which Pascale, through snorts of laughter, translates as "You poor boy." Some small consolation then.

My mother also fails to see the funny side producing her hanky once again as I set about mopping myself down.

Meanwhile, the two Georges have arrived with the order, and once everyone except yours truly has their drinks, Dad stands up and rather pompously proposes a toast to our French friends. This is followed by a clinking of glasses toasted with a

"Cheers." and "A votre santé."

The rest of the evening passes in a merry mix of Dad's anecdotal yarns and Pascale's father's wartime experiences, all of which, with Pascale doing her very best to translate, prove to be entertainment in itself

Very soon, with dusk upon us and a chill wind picking up, we decide it's time to call it a day.

As we rise, Pascale steps forward and plants a delicious kiss on my lips, whispering in my ear that she still has my jacket and will drop it over tomorrow.

With the taste of her lipstick still in my mouth, I

resolve never to clean my teeth again.

Wet trousers aside, I go to bed a very happy boy, enjoying my best night's sleep so far.

THE CARROLLS GO CAMPING 9
(aka Sunset over the Stour)

One very noticeable feature of waking up in a tent is that you can normally determine precisely what the weather is doing outside. If it's windy and raining, the noise on the canvas will inform you it's probably worth staying put.

Conversely, if it's bright sunshine, you will likely be woken early by the feeling that you are in a sauna.

Today the weather being of the latter variety, I am up and out of the tent first, eager to escape my little cocoon and the fetid clammy atmosphere of the tent. The fresh air is certainly invigorating, prompting me to take an early morning stroll along the riverbank.

I make my way over the bridge and down the towpath, choosing on this occasion to follow the river downstream towards the estuary.

It's amazing how much wildlife there is about; within the first few hundred yards, I've already spotted several geese, a family of moorhens, a heron, and even a little water vole.

As I round the next bend, two fishermen are fishing off a small wooden jetty. I pause and enquire whether they had any luck.

"Couple of small eels," one replies, the other one lifting his keep net to show me. I bend forward to observe the wriggling contents.

Must say, I'm not very keen on eels; I definitely wouldn't fancy catching one of those. Fish are a bit slimy, I know, but eels… no thanks!

The further downstream I walk, the wider the river becomes, and shortly I am afforded a view of the sea. Although some way off, it's probably only a couple of miles distant.

The landscape is much more open here, and with very few trees about, it's really quite exposed. With a low mist creeping in, I decide not to venture further, I'm also regretting not having my jacket; best I think to start making my way back.

Returning to the tent, all the family are up and about. Dad is busy doing something with the car, his head buried under the bonnet. Mum has got some breakfast going, the delicious smell of frying bacon reminding me I'm hungry. My sister helping her, looks up and asks where I've been.

"We were getting a bit worried. We thought you might have been kidnapped or something," she says jokingly.

"No, nothing like that, just wanted to check out some more of the river, that's all," I replied.

I tell them about the wildlife, the fishermen's catch, and how close we are to the sea.

"Don't like the sound of those eels," says my sister wrinkling her nose.

"Can't you eat those?" says Dad, briefly appearing from under the bonnet to wipe his hands.

"Think I would prefer bacon," I say.

"Well, if you wash your hands and sit down, this should be ready in a minute," chimes in Mum.

After a hearty al fresco breakfast of bacon and eggs, enjoyed all the more without the presence of the black and yellow perils, it's decided, with the weather set fair, we will head off to the sea once again.

Travelling a little further afield, this time along the north Kent coast, turns out to be a good choice.

We alight upon a beautiful sandy beach which proves Ideal for making sandcastles.

Later as the tide recedes, my sister and I explore the many rock pools, searching for little sea creatures and collecting shells.

Afterwards, picnicking on the large, grassed area above the beach, we congratulate each other on what a superb place we have found.

By late afternoon, my sister and I amuse ourselves playing ball, thus allowing Dad a quick snooze and Mum a chance to have a read. Very soon it's time to be heading back.

Driving over the bridge to the site, I observe the river is now perfectly still with the tide just on the turn. With these ideal conditions likely to prevail for a couple of hours and the weather still deliciously warm, I decided it's a good time to go fishing.

Leaving the others to unpack the car, I quickly gathered my gear and set off along the towpath.

Seeing my favourite spot is unoccupied, I waste no time climbing down the bank and getting settled.

With conditions as they are, it dictates that a float would be the best option. So said, I set about attaching a suitable quill to the line.

Although still not having any decent bait, I have managed to collect the remains of my sister's spam salad.

It may not have appealed to her furry friend, but who knows, maybe the fish might quite like it.

With the river in this calm mode, it certainly is a much easier task to fish. Not having to constantly re-cast makes for a more enjoyable experience, as the float settles in one place, allowing enough time to observe any movement.

After about half an hour without result, save for the interruption of a couple of motorboats and a slow swimming swan, it might be time to try somewhere else along the bank

I am just in the process of reeling in my line when my senses are alerted by the distant uneven throb of a twin-cylinder engine.

Looking up, I see the Panhard crossing over the road bridge.

Strangely my heart starts to beat faster, seemingly in tune with it's irregular engine note.

I put down my rod and watch trance-like as they turn into the carpark and pull up outside their tent.

With a fence and hedge running along the edge of the field, I can't quite see them alight from the car. I can, however, hear their voices as they busy themselves with unloading.

My equilibrium temporarily restored, I set about continuing to fish, this time experimenting with a slightly different type of float.

I know there are fish in this river as I've seen them occasionally rising for flies; either they're very shy, or maybe they just don't fancy spam.

As I have said, I don't think I have the patience for this

hobby. Long periods of concentration are not really my forte.

I resolve to give it about ten more minutes before moving to another spot. After gazing absently for several minutes at the still dark water, my attention is drawn to the sound of footsteps coming over the bridge.

Looking up, I see Pascale.

We exchange waves; my stomach does a tumble.

Knowing she will be arriving very soon, I feel a certain degree of professionalism is called for. So doing, I loose off lots of line and attempt an ambitious cast further upstream. Unfortunately, this only results in me snagging some overhanging trees on the opposite bank.

With the sound of her imminent approach, I frantically set about yanking the line free.

After several sharp tugs, there comes a resounding crack, and the line goes slack, leaving the float dangling mockingly from a low overhanging branch. Immediately I turn to see if she's witnessed my frustrations but luckily, she's still some distance away.

Taking one or two very deep breaths, I put down my rod and, as casually as possible, compose myself for her impending arrival.

Today she is wearing a pretty yellow dress. Also, as

she skips down the bank towards me, I notice she is barefoot.

Treating me to a dazzling smile instantly, making my head swim, she then administers the now familiar French greeting of kisses on both cheeks.

"Bonjour Richard, tu as l'air chaud. You look 'ot, yes?" she says, fanning her face and sitting down next to me.

"Well, yes, I am quite warm now you mention it," I reply.

"You 'ave catch fish?"

"No luck, I'm afraid. Why is your stick not in the water?"

"Stick? Sorry, oh, you mean my rod? Yes, well, slight problem there," I say, pointing to the float hanging limply from the tree.

"Ah, I see it," she says, wrinkling her nose and shielding her eyes with her hand to avoid the low setting sun.

This action draws my attention to a small patch of freckles in the spot just above her cheeks. My stomach takes another lurch.

"Is it your favourite?" she says, pointing to the float.

"Well, actually, I do have another one."

"I can get it for you," she says, standing up.

What occurs next has me totally spellbound. Crossing

her hands over her shoulders, she proceeds to remove her dress, pulling it up and over her head.

I am relieved to see she has a bathing costume on underneath. I think.

Flicking her hair back behind her ears and adjusting her swimsuit to ensure it's prepared for immersion, she delicately steps down the bank to the water's edge.

With just a short hesitation to steady herself, she then suddenly performs an immaculate dive into the river.

Initially, I fear for her safety but soon, witnessing her ability as a swimmer, I am captivated by the spectacle.

After just a few short strokes, she arrives under the errant float, and with a couple of firm yanks, it comes loose.

Confidently treading water, she holds it triumphantly above her head while fixing me a dazzling smile.

I am lost for words.

Again two or three strong strokes and she's climbing up onto the bank like some large velvet otter.

Two more short paces and she stands over me, dripping river water onto my shorts.

I stand up, and she hands me the float like a child might offer a parent a bunch of flowers

We embrace. I'm wet again, but this time, I really don't care.

There follows a brief hiatus as our eyes meet; neither of us is quite sure what to say or do next.

Finally, with what seems like an age, I break the silence with, "When did you learn to swim like that?"

"We 'ave a river near where I live. My father taught me when I was a little girl, three maybe four years old," she replies.

"You had me worried there for a moment," I add. "It was easy as the water is quiet."

"Flat?"

"Calm," I offer.

"Yes, you're right. It is calm, very calm."

I move my fishing gear out of the way and make space for her to sit down next to me. Our shoulders touch, and I start to feel moisture trickling down my arm. Sensing my discomfort, she edges away with an apology.

"I will dry soon. The sun is still warm."

"Don't worry," I say, moving back closer and tentatively putting my arm around her shoulders.

She flashes me a glorious smile, appearing quite happy with this arrangement. So, we remain comfortably like this for some while, gazing at the sultry river as the sun slowly dips down over the roof of *The Dog and Duck*.

This blissful state of affairs is eventually broken by my sister's shrill voice from over in the field, summoning me in for the evening meal.

Pascale turns to me and, giving my hand a tender squeeze, says, "Your sister she is calling. You 'ave to go."

"Yes, I guess so," I say, adding, "Are you coming too?"

"Maybe I will stay 'ear for a while. It is very beautiful."

"Yes, it is. Maybe I'll see you later then," I say, rising and collecting up my fishing gear.

"Yes, maybe," she says."

I make my way up the bank along the towpath and onto the bridge.

On reaching the middle, I stop and look back across to where she sits. Somehow she senses me watching her and gives me a little wave before turning her gaze back towards the slow-moving river.

Back at the campsite, Mum is putting the finishing touches to a soup while Dad's fiddling with the guy-ropes, checking their tension.

"Any luck lad, catch anything?" he asks.

"Only a French girl," my sister replies.

Dad gives me his raised eyebrow expression before

saying, "Probably a lot more interesting than fishing."

After our meal and with darkness drawing in, we retire to our tents.

Dad tries hard to concentrate on his book while my sister and I attempt to swat mosquitoes that have infiltrated during the day.

Observing our feeble efforts, he says the only way to get rid of them is to smoke them out and proceeds to light his pipe.

The tent soon fills with the rich smell of his Bruno Rough tobacco, "the preferred choice for the serious smoker," so it states on the tin.

The fug soon gets too much even for Dad, resulting in a frantic rush to open the tent flaps to allow in some fresh air. This operation leads me to cast doubt as to whether we've successfully got rid of the mosquitoes or just allowed more in.

Eventually, after much coughing, the air clears sufficiently for us all to zip up our sleeping bags, settle down and get some sleep.

THE CARROLLS GO CAMPING 10
(aka Au Revoir au Guttet)

The morning dawns bright, sunny, and still very warm.

As it's the penultimate day of our holiday Mum and Dad ask us how we would like to spend it.

My sister wants to return to our newfound beach. I'm harbouring other ideas, but so as not to cause any disagreements, I defer to her wishes.

Thus, it is we enjoy another agreeable day at the beach doing much the same activities as on our previous visit.

Like the day before, by mid-afternoon, we are all ready to head back to the campsite.

"Shall we do a spot of fishing after tea?" says Mum as we approach the bridge. I'm just about to respond to her request. When pulling into the carpark, my attention is drawn to the field.

My heart misses a beat.

Where there were three tents in the field, now there are just two. Our two.

"Looks like they've gone," says my sister blandly, looking to me for a reaction.

To shocked to respond, I remotely climb from the car and make my way slowly over to where their tent stood.

I inspect the ground, gently brushing my foot across the yellowed patch of grass. As if doing so might somehow miraculously conjure up it's sudden reappearance.

My reverie is broken by my mother calling me. Turning, I see her holding up my jacket.

Dejectedly, I make my way across the field to join them.

"It was just hanging here," she says, pointing to the top of the tent pole. "At least she remembered to return it," she adds, handing me the jacket. I slip it on.

Distracted, I mutter, "I'm just going for a stroll along the river."

"Don't go too far, will you? I'm just going to fix us some tea," I hear her say as I quietly walk away.

Walking up the slope to cross over the bridge, I notice a cool breeze has sprung up. Instinctively, I pull up my jacket collar and automatically put my hands in the pockets.

My right hand touches a small slip of paper. I withdraw a note.

"Merci,"	{Thank you,}
"Mon-Ami Richard."	{My friend Richard.}
"Avec Amour,"	{With Love,}
"Pascale."	{Pascale.}

XXXX

Reaching the middle of the bridge, I stop and re-read her brief message.

Looking down into the fast-flowing river, I consider just for a moment tearing it up and dropping it like confetti into the water.

Thankfully, the moment passes. Instead, I fold it neatly, carefully placing it back in my pocket, before taking a final slow walk back across the bridge to the campsite

My sister sensing my disposition, attempts to lift my spirits by offering to join her in dispatching a few wasps.

I respectfully decline her offer, preferring my own company just now. I quietly adjourn to our tent.

Later over our meal and with the last day of our holiday behind us, I can sense the mood in the camp is a bit down. Dad, as usual, does his best to change this by telling us some jokes.

He gets a few laughs, but very soon, the weather has the

last say, with a constant drizzle setting in, prematurely and somewhat fittingly putting an end to our day

The weather continues to do it's worst during the night, keeping us all awake with the wind flapping the canvas and occasionally whistling right through the tent.

There's not much improvement in the morning either, making breaking camp an unpleasant task for us all.

After much strenuous effort, we eventually get all the camping equipment stowed onboard the Morris, once again restoring it's sporting stance. Soon we are moving out across the car park up onto the road.

I take a glance out the back window, silently mouthing a quiet "Au revoir…"

We steadily make our way back home the way we came, the rain now intensifying once again.

The car's windscreen wipers create a hypnotic effect as they gallantly do their best to deal with the deluge.

Transfixed by their movement, I ponder what this holiday has taught me. It really has been a voyage of discovery.

One, I've discovered I still like cricket.

Two, I've discovered I don't like camping.

Three, I've discovered I don't care much for fishing. And last and probably the most important of all...

I've discovered I really do quite like girls.

Printed in Great Britain
by Amazon